echo designs

her way out

of a paper bag

a book about how to change anything by
using design thinking (& *storytelling!*)

storylab®

BetaTest edition published by **story**lab® in 2019
Book designed, researched, and edited by **story**lab® + jack roberts in association with Parsons School of Design in Paris and NYC.
Chief Editor: Mark Swift. Narrative Designer: Jack Roberts
The Library of Congress has catalogued the trade paperback American BETA edition as follows:
Roberts, Jack.
Echo Designs Her Way Out of a Paper Bag/Jack Roberts – BETA Ed.
Originally published: NY, NY. ©2019
ISBN 978-1-946278-18-0 (pbk.)
ISBN 978-1-946278-20-3 (cloth)
ISBN 978-1-946278-21-0 (Kindle)
ISBN 978-1-946278-19-7 (audio)
LCCN: 201-9-943-565

an

inspiring quote:

"there is nothing more powerful

than an idea whose time

has come."

victor hugo

(it's a classic move to
start with an inspiring quote)

content(s):

tip:

dust off those dreams

it is the proverbial go time

side note:

this volume

has many

tips and

side notes

my

first

rodeo

"This ain't my first rodeo," the cowboy said, as he checked out my mom's ass, then slapped it. He wore all black and a wire brace on his face.

My Cherokee mother looked at him.

He repeated: "T'ain't my farst rodeo."

I'd heard him clearly the first time. She heard him clearly the second. He sounded worse the second time to me. Two weeks earlier, his face had been stepped on by a bull at the actual rodeo. In this case, though, he was making my Native American mother some "far bread" that he'd learned from an "Injun" fellow in New Mexico.

Later, I'd write a character based on this guy. For now, at 5 years of age, I just stood there staring up at the grease crackling in the iron skillet, the brace on his face, and the fact that in my kitchen there was a cowboy, an Indian, and me—a bit of both.

He looked over at me and attempted a smile. If you've never seen someone smile with a metal brace on his face after a bull-riding mishap, you should get out more. I don't remember his name. I'm not sure my mother would either.

My parents had recently divorced and now there was a stranger with a metal face in my new-old and much smaller kitchen. My mother had made fry bread many times, it was epic, and she was, too. One helluva storyteller and a designer in her own way—that one.

Still, perhaps the loneliness of her recent divorce humored him or maybe it was simply sorrow for his reconstructed face. Humor him she did.

He asked me if I wanted something. I pretended I didn't understand him. I liked watching him strain under the effort. I was a mumbler by nature and so even though he spoke my native tongue of quiet, I feigned on.

"Do you want somfun?"

I saw my chance and I struck. "Some fun?" I said. "I sure do. I love fun. Want to play cowboys and Indians?" I asked.

My ever-sharp mother smirked behind him at me as she used the distraction to secretly turn the oil down. Otherwise, it would not be cooked inside. She was careful to let this stranger have his glory. I was not.

The man in black continued: "I said," (struggle, struggle) "some fing! Can I *help* you?"

"Can you answer a question for me since it isn't your first rodeo?" I said, while my mother fidgeted behind me and turned his "far" bread over in the cast iron skillet, the one I'd have to clean later.

The cowboy-toy shrugged, and his metal brace went askew. He didn't seem to notice the dangling antenna jutting out of the analog television that was his face. So, I pretended not to as well and went on, "Does anyone ever have a *first* rodeo?" I asked.

He laughed until it hurt, which didn't take long. I left the room as they shooed me away. "Funny kid ..." I heard.

My mother exclaimed, likely to change the subject, "Well, would you look at that, it's coming out perfect."

"Told you wasn't *my farst*," was the smug reply. She can't be serious, I thought, as I went upstairs to check on my younger brother. I was serious, though, and I still am. This thing we do as humans …

When is it *ever* anybody's first rodeo?

I get it, we seem to like to seem to already know a thing or two. It's embarrassing to be on the outs of anything, even knowledge. In its simplest form, our pride is likely a defense mechanism making sure we aren't robbed of something. We desperately don't want to be taken advantage of by people that seem to be in the know more than we are. As I age or fail forward, what I notice happening when we do this, is that we end up taking advantage of ourselves. We shut down the optimum learning cycle. We stunt our growth.

We move away from the power of vulnerability, the growth mindset, the beginner's mind, the blank slate, the open heart, and the list goes on. We have a ba-gillion phrases to connect on this topic, some of which hold concepts that represent whole movements in human culture. But they all kind of mean the same thing, in a way. Or at least, if different, they seem to call to a state of human receptivity to the living world around us. Even as I storytell, I observe the tendency in myself. I have never written about the transformative power of **storytelling** when **combined with design thinking**. Let's call it **narrative design.**

Narrative design isn't in the dictionary. At least not the Merriam-Webster. It's in my glossary of terms at the end of this book and it is on Wikipedia, though. It's a relatively newer role in video game design mostly in the role-playing game (RPG) world. It's not the writer.

The focus of the narrative designer is to design the *narrative elements* of the game. Then, after that, to champion the story within the development of the process, including championing the game writer. So, it's a little different. Maybe a little more strategic and over-arching given that the role is really about architecting the story we live and not necessarily controlling what happens in that story. Don't worry, this isn't a video game book.

Instead, it's a hybrid book of fiction and non-fiction (which I think all books in some way are…) that explains how to change anything, even your life, with a combo package of design thinking and storytelling (narrative design).

It's been said that design thinking is a bridge from us to our purpose. If that's the case, storytelling is the person using the bridge and creating a life. The two when combined are explosive, ripe for action, and primed for momentum. There are few things I like better than momentum, except maybe the smell of beeswax candles and the taste of toaster waffles.

That's what this book is about: creating momentum. But to do that, we need tools and frameworks on what to do and how to do it. There are lots of other books on *why*. This won't spend much time on that topic. Instead, it will focus on *how* we uncover *what* is called for right now, or go about creating what's next.

We're mostly through the Informational Age and there are crazy amounts of uncountable data on what we can do and should do in life and in the world to make both better. We have so much data it's scary. We have data on everything and everyone and all things tangible. But we have data intangibles, too, like love and empathy and sociopathy and more. Now, *what* do we do with all this stuff, all this data, all this knowledge, all this information? *How* do we gather all the *what* and make some *hows*?

Listen, as I mentioned, I'm Cherokee. When I was a kid, other kids used to walk up and say "how" when they'd see my mom at drop-off. They were mostly being playful. And though that was regrettably insensitive, it was also before empathy became something other than a sign of weakness or an artistic sensibility. It was a time before we knew *how* to do what should be done. It's going to take some courage for us to live the dreams we know are ours to live once we look upon them after the death of our assumptions.

side note:

did you know that

how in that context

came from the lakota

sioux word for greeting?

it was spelled "hau."

The side note brings up an interesting point, because in Hollywood where I now make film and television—it was applied to every Native American tribe. We have to resist the urge to oversimplify and apply the factory-line mentality of the Industrial Age to our present social situation.

Instead, we must embrace the collated data and its continual findings in a hyper-localized way, and that's starting to happen in societal solutionism. In urban markets, you can have any restaurant deliver food. New businesses can print leather messenger bags in their garage and sell them around the world. People can run entire global publishing companies from their laptop in a lower-cost-of-living city.

We run into trouble when we go back to the Industrial Age mindsets of a cog in the wheel or a factory line worker or of an employee stuck in their office cubicle after the truth of our Information Age has set us free. But set us free for what? Maybe to implement, to make something of ourselves and our lives in real time or online. But … how? Again with the how!

This brings us to our next age, or maybe just our next stage of human evolution, the *Age of How*. I like design thinking mixed with storytelling as the system creating the next solution. But, maybe we should begin with a primer on "design thinking" as a methodology before we toss my hybridization into the mix.

I forget most have no familiarity with it because it's in my everyday. I'm design thinking for clients, books, movies, tv, and my classroom at Parsons School of Design. Design thinking is not yet in the public sphere in a common way. A big reason for that is that designers are often like the Kung-Fu masters that were angry at Bruce Lee for wanting to share martial arts with the world. It's understandable. People often get protective of our deeper ways of being, the things that we perceive make us unique or special.

I've this hunch though, that becoming special is less about what you do and more about the person you are while doing it. To that end, I'm going to let you in on the design way, the engine behind how to create "how's" that we as creators and designers call strategic design or more commonly, "design thinking." It's also the base subject of this book. I've iterated design thinking and/or built upon it by infusing storytelling techniques. I wanted to know how we can make wisdom out of our knowledge.

Okay, so, what is "design thinking?" Intangibly, it's a five (and *sometimes six) step but infinite process of never being done and always being better. Tangibly, it's a way of making things, improving things, fixing things, and innovating nearly anything. Most companies and people that use it are designers or strategic designers and most often it's used as a way to solve problems and change things for the better. The five (and *sometimes six) steps of design thinking are:

1) *empathize:* Learn about the humans for whom you are creating.

2) *design:* Have an opinion or a point of view based on insights from studying the humans for whom you are creating.

3) *ideate:* Brainstorm and flood your world with creative ideas that can serve your humans from your point of view.

4) *prototype:* Build something, anything, that tangibly represents one or more of your ideas that serve your humans best.

5) *test:* Return to your original humans for whom you are creating and test your ideas for their feedback.

6) **reiterate:* Rapidly adapt to new insights and create new realities by moving through steps 1 through 5 again.

So, that's the paraphrased summation of design thinking. It's a process that once mastered can be used to solve any problem, create any solution, and build pretty much anything. If you need a tangible example consider tech giant Apple and their phones. They've never released anything but a prototype they are testing on us. What design thinking doesn't always and easily do, is help us make sense of the world, change cultures, and create meaning for us. But, that's the subject of this book, that is where my hybrid of narrative design® steps in with storytelling.

How do we make sense of all this information, of all this data? How do we move from intangible to tangible again, invisible to visible? There's a way and it's by design but it's not only design. It's also through the narrative we are weaving and the story we are living. This is why I my work revolves around infusing design thinking with storytelling techniques. That way we move beyond problem solving and into designing brand new realities together. We co-create places where our problems simply vanish because the reality has been changed. It's been rewritten.

My friends we are on the cusp of the next. We are in the Internet of Things, ideas are hitting rapid prototyping faster than ever before and hyper-localizing like never before. The human race is taking another breath, she's contracting to expand. That's a great thing. It means we are alive and breathing. I've written this book, this journey and it's a hybrid, too, a prototype.

We will move in and out of a fiction novella and a non-fiction, change-anything book, all right here. I think truth is best delivered in story form. You see, I've ghostwritten non-fiction books and often found them, well, boring. I've written fiction books and award-winning screenplays in film and television, but often found them not taken as seriously as their gravity intended.

We will mostly follow Echo, our lead character, throughout her journey to becoming a narrative designer, a strategic designer, design thinker, or simply a designer of life. But I'll also share and expound nuggets of hard-learned wisdom like an easy-listening station in the elevator on the way to where you are going. Basically, I'm doing a mash-up for the very first time. So, in a way...

this is my first rodeo.

I trust you to forgive my shortcomings, cyclical thinking, or easy-listening-ness as I attempt to be relentlessly helpful in a world that's currently changing faster than we are.

Brené Brown likes to say there's an immense power in vulnerability. I tend to concur enough to follow up that agreement with my time and energy. It's always a vulnerable undertaking to write a book and share it with others. Maybe, just maybe, if we are lucky (*yes, I'm superstitious, all former baseball players are*) we could find vulnerable power in this together?

I just hope my face doesn't get stepped on.

1.

echo

goes

dreamcatching

"you never really understand a person until

you consider things from his (or her) point

of view"

harper lee

1.

Humans are my spirit animal.

In spite or maybe because of the fact that we are all a little bipolar. It's our safety net. We call it good and bad, right and wrong, black and white, with us or against us, cheese or no cheese, and the list goes on.

Nevertheless, I am in love with us. I love what humans can do when we remember we can do anything. I love who we become when we allow the gray matter of our brains to accept the gray areas in life and create great things for people, planet, and profit anyway.

Our drawbacks, our stress responses, and our brokenness are too obvious to call out here, and yet, in some ways, that's just how we do. Maybe, if we could accept the shadow, we could better direct the light. That's how it is in lighting design on a film or TV set.

Humans are chaos incubators so that we can be order creators. It's all very thrilling. I'm anxious to see what we become when we grow up.

It's this mentality the *either/or* mindset, that's helped us build the first part of the human experience. It's the two-way street mental model that created the two-way street, literally. It's an infrastructure and exoskeleton builder. It's great to build with and grow with … to a point. By itself it's not enough to reach full human buy-in. Something in us knows we are more than an animal. Something in us knows we have dreams. The *either/or* paradigm doesn't build dreams, people do. And people are not so simple. We are not so black and white. Our brains matter is not called black and white matter for a reason.

Several months ago, I had the pleasure of being asked to write an article for a publication out of London. They wanted a piece on the Information Age and what it meant for the future of storytelling in media now that data could show us what stories people wanted. They weren't super happy with me because I wrote that the Information Age and the age of data is on its deathbed because it has made us and trains us to be primarily reactive to what has come before instead of focusing on designing what's next. I like the quote attributed to Henry Ford: "If I had asked people what they wanted, they would have said faster horses." He means a faster horse instead of a car … a car.

If that were a metaphor, where are our cars today? I'll give you a hint: not in the data. Instead, my experience and my hunch is that the proverbial "cars" of the future will be in *what* we see in the data, what we do with the data, and in *how* we use it or create with it. Ford knew what people meant by saying they wanted a faster horse. He knew that they wanted to get where they were going faster. That was the real data. The *assumption* is that we needed a horse.

Assumptions are a dead giveaway to the *either/or* mentality. Either a horse or walking … or a horse or a *faster* horse … nowhere was an option that didn't involve what we didn't already know. But to plan for that un-reality feels chaotic and to create with it in mind feels downright unsafe. Nevertheless, that's the way of the emerging paradigm that can and does move as quickly as the ever-shifting sands of today's society.

I was working with a genius of a shapeshifter for about a year on a book project about the end of an American era. We were researching, writing, and designing a world conveying the fall of one culture into another. This shapeshifter I was narrative designing for is a man who could have been any age with his ability to be present in any scenario, with any age group, and in any conversation. He's been called a shaman by many around him for the way he artfully architects the delivery of wisdom in practice for Fortune 50 leaders around the globe.

I observed him carefully as he absorbed the world around him, even my limited wisdom and understanding of narrative, design, and story. I watched in awe as he could always contribute consciously, calmly when called for and passionately when needed, and add real value to any situation with any person.

We did some deeply personal narrative design work for him, recalling these stories that he'd lived through to create this project together regarding a period of his life. The book ended up changing us both. He taught me about what it means to be in your 70s and maintaining an active growth mindset.[1] He told me that I taught

---

[1] Dweck, Carol S. (2008). *Mindset: The New Psychology of Success.* New York: Ballantine Books.

him about the real meaning of faith. It was and remains an epic exchange all around.

However, I don't feel like I taught him anything about faith. I simply said what I saw in him. I told him that I think it takes immense faith to practice anything but self-preservation here on earth. Even more to believe in humanity despite the odds against us, and then a certain creative faith and confidence to engage in this experiment we have here on earth called society. This re-storied[i] his narrative.

I've never seen another human being so incredibly comfortable with the inherent tension that life holds for each of us. This is the comfortability in the ambiguous that I believe we must cultivate to effect true change. There's a certain philosophy of embrace or acceptance to it. I think it's the way we leave behind our bipolar tendency as humans. To catch our dreams, we need it, and to build our dreams we will need it and more. We will call this new mindset a *"yes/and"*[ii] mindset.

I first encountered the *yes/and* mentality in childhood. We all did. It's on the playground. You'll never see a better example of it than children playing together for hours in a park only to be asked by their parents later, "What's your new friend's name?"

A shrug followed by "I don't know" is often the reply. This is because both parties utterly accepted one another. The play was a series of games that built upon each other in a way that kept them co-creating for hours. This is why there's such a large play movement in business right now. Stuart Brown wrote a book on this that kicked off a corporate movement.[2]

I think much of it can be boiled down to the *yes/and* paradigm. After the playground, it's something I next encountered in improvisational comedy, which I've practiced for over twenty-five years now. In a way it's about creating a brainstorming session where there's comfortability in the "creative process" (← read: CHAOS). Anyone that tells you otherwise is selling something. Now, don't get me wrong, you can design narrative structures to facilitate the

---

[2] Brown, S. L., & Vaughan, C. C. (2009). *Play: How It Shapes theBrain, Opens the Imagination, and Invigorates the Soul*. New York: Avery.

chaos, but if it's not scary, you're not doing it right.

There's a certain "all-in-ness" to the whole thing. A vital piece that is often forgotten in moving your mindset to the *yes/and* is letting go. We tend as facilitators, educators, creative directors, chief executives, and leaders to forget that acceptance doesn't happen if letting go isn't also occurring at the same time. I don't know about you, but I've been in many a brainstorming session where people say the words "*yes/and*" and are actually saying "no, you're wrong" as a "build."

Which is silly.

They are being a silly goose.[iii]

side note:

i want to bring

back the phrase

"silly goose"

Loads of mystics have methods for letting go. There are even children's songs about it of Broadway quality (*thank you, Idina*[3]). Many religions build their pillars with this kind of stone. I don't see it like that, though. I think it's just as easy to make an *either/or* out of concepts like letting go or even acceptance. When the religions and their mystics teach it, form must give way to non-form. And moving from form to formless is just another two-way street, just another *either/or* mindset prevailing.

I'm advocating doing something else.

I'm suggesting that we use empathy to humanize ourselves and others. This will take us from an *either/or* to the beginning of a *yes/and*. It's also the first stage of the design thinking process, *empathizing*.[iv] I see empathizing a little differently in the narrative design space, that is, where design thinking meets storytelling. I see it as "dreamcatching."[v]

My grandmother gave me a dreamcatcher at a powwow when I was a kid. I took it home, unwrapped its leather straps, defeathered it, took

[3] Idina Menzel, "Let It Go." (2013)

the beads off, and unstrung it. I wanted to see if I could make one, too. I slept with it under my pillow as I slowly reconstructed it in a ridiculous but artful manner. Design is messy.

I slept with nightmares for years.

The purpose of a dreamcatcher is a night-time security system for our dreams. They are supposed to filter out the dreams that build us from those that destroy us. I'd disassembled mine. Yikes. (I told you I was superstitious.) In other words, it's a way of filtering our subconscious ideas.

And just so we are careful not to dive headlong into a "dream *either/or*" mentality, let's define "build" and "destroy." Build, we will call constructive, meaning it gives us more than it takes from us. This is important because it doesn't mean there's not pain, or hardship, just ultimately that it gives us more than it takes from us.

We will say that destroy is essentially destructive and we will define destructive as something that takes more than it gives. Kudos to Dr. David R. Hawkins for the constructive/destructive definitions.[4] So, then, the purpose of dreamcatching as we will use it will be in the sense of the first stage of the narrative design process (design thinking hybridized with storytelling), empathizing. But we will do it a little differently than in the design thinking process because instead of going out and doing design research on a customer base or a user or even an audience member, we are starting on an individual's mindset as she lives out her assumptions.

Our assumptions lead to our actions and create our biases, and these little buggers make certain that we look for research to support what we already suspect. It's a sure way to never empathize, stay in an *either/or*, and also never make any real friends in life. Sorry, for that last one … just thought you should know.

tip:

know empathy, know friends
no empathy, no friends.

---

[4] *Force: The Hidden Determinants of Human Behavior*. Carlsbad, CA: Hay House.

side note:

i might still

be your friend.

(i have been known

to hang on too long.)

Let's take a look at assumptions, creative confidence, acceptance, and moving from an *either/or* to a *yes/and* in order to empathize in this little slice of Echo's life. Maybe you'll see someone you know.

← side note:

actual pic of

the design processes

starts fine, gets messy, ends well

Echo left her house this morning in plenty of time. She didn't want to call her boyfriend. She'd been calling him too often. She could feel a tension growing between them that made her uncomfortable.

She was just finishing up her second shift at the Waffle House. Echo had planned to run home before the second shift to pick up her change of clothes, her improv clothes, her nice clothes, the "performance" clothes. That plan was crap and she knew it was crap when she made it. But, *classic Echo*, she'd betrayed herself again. If only she'd learned not to betray herself like it said in *Leadership and Self-Deception*.[5] She had to stay "out of the box."

In the last year, since skipping the offered college scholarship in favor of moving with her "man" to this Podunk town, she'd become fascinated with business books. She'd always been a voracious reader. It's an introverted-and-painfully-shy

---

[5] The Arbinger Institute (2018). *Leadership and Self-Deception: Getting Out of the Box*. Oakland, CA: Berrett-Koehler.

person's must. All she has to do is learn to listen to that weird, small voice inside and she just knows she'll live the dreams, all the dreams … but she doesn't. It's just not that simple.

I mean, she has before, like when against her natural inclinations she took a job waiting tables and joined an improv troupe. She'd read about action-oriented new habits being what can change you from the outside>inside in *The Power of Habit*.[6]

Lately she'd been questioning these decisions. She'd been questioning every decision. *It's like that when you betray yourself*, she thought. *Everything just feels really off and you're not sure why.* She'd never been very decisive despite reading the full-of-amazing-research-and-info book called *Decisive*.[7] She never *felt* decisive.

Instead, Echo looks down at her phone for the third time, wondering again if she should call her boyfriend to ask for help, still undecided. Her manager, Pete, looks at her over his dirty

---

[6] Duhigg, C. (2012). *The Power of Habit: Why We Do What We Do and How to Change*. Toronto: Doubleday Canada.

[7] Heath, C., & Heath, D. (2014). *Decisive: How to Make Better Decisions in Life and Work*. London: Random House Books.

fingernails, that he can't stop biting, and nods for her to put the phone away. The way he stares at her, no, the way that he stares at everyone, is a little like he's still at home playing *Magic: The Gathering*, and you're just a character in his story.

That's funny, Echo thinks to herself, as she mindlessly grabs the coffee pot with the faded orange rim off the burner and pours another cup for that decaf customer at table eight. *I wonder how I can work that in tonight?* Her phone buzzes in her pocket.

She excuses herself to the restroom to take the call, knowing that Fingernail Pete is staring at her ass as she walks away. She's used to that from people. She has a nice ass. At first it was flattering, then affronting, and now she feels relatively indifferent about it. *Is it healthy to feel indifferent?* she wonders, as she locks the door, pulls out her phone and answers it. It's him. He called her, *that's a great sign.*

"Honey, I was going to call you," she whispered.

"Why are you whispering?" he asked.

She wonders why he has a habit of speaking louder every time she whispers.

She shoves down the small voice inside her mentioning that this dude would be a total shit to travel with and that she loves travel. Bill Bryson says it's vital to have the right travel partners.[8]

She tries to tell him why she's whispering in a low voice and he raises his volume to cut her off. Whispering annoys the shit out of him, he tells her. It nags at her because it negates the whole reason that she's whispering in the first place. She doesn't want to be heard at work.

She tells him this in a slightly louder whisper. He doesn't quieten much and still sounds frustrated with her to boot. "About tonight, I'm not coming. I've been to your shows several times and honestly, I just need to recoup from my day."

She wilts.

She echoes what he says, "just need to recoup from my day?"

---

[8] Bryson, B. (2002). *Walkabout: A Walk in the Woods, Down Under*. London: Doubleday.

"That's what I just said, Echo. Don't be so prosaic."

"Prosaic?"

"Case in point, Echo, echo, echo ..." he says.

Someone knocks at the door.

"Well, can you at least bring my clothes by? That way I don't have to just play a waitress on the stage tonight."

With the silence on the other end of the line, the second knock at the door sounds even louder.

"What's that noise?" he finally asks, agitated.

"I'm in the bathroom," she whispers lower still.

He gets louder, "You know I can't hear you when you whisper like that! It's like you don't even care about how my ears work. So selfish, Echo."

Now, it's her turn to be silent. She mutes her phone to him, before shouting to the person at the door, "Just a minute! Almost done."

She hears him on the phone, "Echo, I'll bring your stupid clothes up to the theater."

She whispers back to the muted phone, forgetting that she had placed it on mute. He gets even louder, like secretly Echo knows he one day will in a foreign country, like when a Frenchman can't speak English in response to him. Somehow, in his feeble mind, his loudness will equate with speaking another language.

Volume isn't another language, a-hole, she thinks. She unmutes the phone as he's repeating himself. She whispers loudly into the phone to stop him from hanging up after this tirade, "I'm here, sorry, I didn't realize I had you on mute. I'm in the bathroom."

Silence. He chuckles into the phone. "The bathroom? I'll bring your clothes to the theater, but I'm not staying." He chuckles again. "Bathroom."

Now, she's trying not to laugh as the absurdity of her own scenario dawns on her. The door handle jiggles, the universal sign to hustle to the person inside. *Yep, still locked*, she thinks.

"I can hear the door jiggling, that's hysterical!" His chuckle graduates to a laugh.

"Stop laughing, the doors are thin, they'll hear you," she tells him.

The handle jiggles again and there's another knock, firmer this time, a knock without fingernails. *Oh, shit.*

"Echo, is ... is ... how do I say this ... is everything alright in there? What I mean to say is, you've been in there an awfully long time and this kind lady out here has been waiting."

She hears someone whispering to Fingernail Pete. He hesitantly continues, "And she says she thinks you're on your phone. That you are taking a phone call and not going to the bathroom."

Echo sits down on the closed lid of the toilet. "Oh, shit," she whispers into the phone. His laugh on the other end has now turned into side-splitting guffaws.

"Echo, are you laughing at me? I don't want to pull this card," (*Magic: The Gathering card*, she thinks) Fingernail Pete says, "but I am the boss of you."

She quickly hangs up the phone. He calls back immediately while she's trying to think. She hangs up again just as fast.

Think fast, think fast, think fast …

"Well, this isn't a laughing matter." Fingernail Pete is perturbed. *Think fast, Echo, think fast …*

"I'm farting!" she blurted out, and covered her mouth as though she could shove the words back in and trap them somehow.

Silence settled just outside the bathroom. She fought back a laugh as she thought, *imagine that, a-hole, the next time you look at my ass.*

"F-f-farting?" he can't even say it. "And you expect that I don't know the difference between a f-f-fart and laughter?"

She knew she had him on the ropes by this point, *go hard or go home*. She leaned in and continued, "Sometimes, Pete, a woman has to laugh to get the poop out."

Silence led to longer silence.

Oh, wait! I can laugh now, Echo realized.

She started laughing and couldn't stop.

Echo then looked at the time. She was now off work.

She flushed the toilet and washed her hands. She hit the automatic dryer and looked at herself in the mirror, and then chose instead to dry her hands off in styling her wayward hair.

Echo walked out of the restroom and saw only an old lady exiting the men's restroom behind her. Echo turned left and clocked out with the old punchcard system. She began to untie her apron to leave it, but noted it needed to be washed. Tomorrow was laundry day anyway, so she kept it on.

As she walked past the register, Pete was hiding behind his fingernails. She met him head-on, saying, "Goodnight, Pete."

He barely nodded to her and, sure enough, she didn't feel his eyes on her backside as she walked out the glass door and across the street to the theater.

She felt oddly free as she approached the old double doors to head inside. She doubled back and hit up the box office, "Hey there, did anyone leave a bag of clothes up here for me? It would have been an old messenger bag."

The man with the epic sideburns just shook his head and shrugged. Echo went inside. She looked down at her phone to check the time and noticed a text from her boyfriend: "CHECK YOUR VM."

She listened to it on her way into the old cinema—that's what it was, an old cinema with a stage on it. Once a month, this small-town improv troupe got together to give the audience a good time with their ability to roll with whatever. Echo stopped and tried calling him. His phone went straight to his person-less generic voicemail message, "The person at 424-771- … is not available." *No, he didn't just ignore my call.*

Mike, a large and bearded man in overalls who's hysterical, walks by Echo and waves. She hardly sees him. Her boyfriend's message explained tersely that he wasn't coming and that she can play a waitress tonight since that's all she'll ever be anyway and seeing as her job is so all-important to her that she can hang up on him.

As she heads backstage, the rest of the cast is in the green room and people, especially the significant others of the other cast members, are beginning to fill the audience.

"It's going to be a packed night," Mike says, to no one in particular. He raises his eyebrows at Echo and motions to her Waffle House waitress uniform, saying, "Great costume."

"Now, I can only be a waitress," she says, near tears.

Mike shakes his head. "You will always be a waitress, my dear." Echo starts crying.

"Nice one," calls Jade from across the room. Jade comes over to comfort and hug Echo.

Mike pulls them both into his huge wingspan. "I wasn't finished, ladies. I was saying,"—he takes a breath to make the thought count—"that you will always be a waitress, you are everything you've ever been and ever will be, and a waitress is simply one of those many things. What's the first rule of improv, Echo?"

"Yes … and," Echo said, "Yes, and."

Echo went on to slay the house that night, as she reenacted the bathroom scene to the laughter of a hundred people. At the night's end, when each performer stepped up to take a bow, Echo's cheer was a standing ovation.

Mike, in the story above, illustrated a valuable point. We are all of the things. Sure, she was a waitress. And she always would be. Yes, and … she's an improv actress … yes, and she's a woman that's learning to listen to that small voice

… yes, and, she's reading like a maniac and inside a sincere growth mindset … yes, and she's yet to realize her worth and surround herself accordingly …! You get the idea. She's all the things and so are we, all the things we ever were.

Madeleine L'Engle is the author of the *A Wrinkle in Time* series of books, and many others, even some mystical ones, like *Walking on Water*,[9] where she discusses being able to walk up the stairs without touching the floor as a young girl until someone told her it was impossible. Maddy says it like this when she's asked about how she can write a 14-year-old girl so well; she tells the interviewer that she was a 14-year-old girl. She also happened to be a 20-year-old girl and a 30-something girl and a 48-year-old girl, too.

We are all of the things.

We can shapeshift if we know this, we can become the change we want to see in our lives. But we must begin in the *yes/and*-mindset. I see the *yes/and*-mindset as the first part of the

---

[9] L'Engle, M. (2016). *Walking on Water: Reflections on Faith and Art*. New York: Convergent Books.

dreamcatcher; I think starting in the dreamcatcher is a good beginning.

The *yes/and* mindset begins with acceptance. We must fundamentally accept ourselves, our own ideas/voices, and then we are able to easily accept others. This doesn't mean we don't discern. We just don't judge. What's the difference? A judgment assigns value – *either/or* to something – the good/bad paradigm. Discernment simply decides if something is for me or not at this time.

It's just not as intense as all that "This is right! And this is wrong!" stuff. The dreamcatcher accepts every dream that comes through, but it holds some back and lets some in based on what we need and what we don't to serve what we are trying to accomplish.

So, we are going to journey with Echo into the dreamcatcher.[10] Maybe she'll notice that small voice inside and grow still enough to hear it.

Be warned: this can get messy. The design process and the story process both are a chaos

---

[10] *storylab* is the design lab dedicated to the power of story in the world. Discover more of their exercises at storylab.tv

before they are a straight line. I think another word for chaos might be ambiguity. It makes us wiggle. But learning to live in empathy means learning to hold the tension between polarity. Did you know that many psychologists and their schools of thought, though they differ on many things, tend to agree on one? It's often seen as the sign of maturation in adult development, the tolerance for ambiguity. The more comfortable we become in the mess of life, the ambiguity, the more we are able to hear the small voice and this exercise, the dreamcatcher, can be a good start.

It's like an empathy map had a baby with a polarity map and it forms the basis of catching the dreams of those we create for and our own. Let's meet up again with Echo.

Echo pulled into the driveway of her duplex late that night. It had been an epic performance for her, by far her best turn in ever. She was really feeling like she was growing into this improvisation thing. *Not bad for an introvert.* It was hard to fathom that she'd only gotten into it for the same reason she got into waiting tables—that she was painfully, dreadfully shy.

No one would know it now, for sure, and the truth of the matter was that she was, in fact, still incredibly timid. She didn't often say what was on her mind and certainly didn't share what was going on in her heart and soul. She sat with the car engine turned off, listening to the end of the song on her Spotify station. She was singing along to the music wonderfully in her head. To an onlooker, though, she would have looked nearly asleep with her hands at ten and two.

She could see the blue light of the television on in the duplex and, judging by the jumpy nature of its flicker, her heart-throb was video gaming with some *Call of Duty*. *Ironic name*, she thought, *great game for someone so dutiful*.

She unplugged the phone as the song ended and sat in the quiet. She looked at the little dreamcatcher hanging from her rearview mirror. She tried to think of where she got it. *A flea market, maybe?* She flicked it with her finger and watched it move back and forth, then sway slowly from side to side.

Was it just her or did she feel something when she touched it? Static electricity, maybe.

She flicked it again and was certain she felt something this time. It was like the little dreamcatcher had touched her the exact same moment she had touched it. *But that's not possible, that's ...*

Suddenly, she could hear Big Mike's bearded voice, "What's the first rule of improv?"

Yes, And ...

She could now feel the rocking and swaying of the little trinket as it moved back and forth. It seemed to be communicating with her in its movement. She'd read about this sort of thing, hypnotism. There'd even been a hypnotist at her high school, during senior year. He asked for volunteers and she hadn't been picked. She also hadn't raised her hand, even though she found the whole thing fascinating.

Her thoughts went back to the *flea market, no ... where did this come from ...* as she drifted deeper into the web of the dreamcatcher and her eyes inadvertently closed.

"Yes, and." She'd stated it out loud and said it before she'd been called on. Wait, her hand was up. *What the...*

Echo looked around the classroom. Yes, a classroom and a pretty hot professor. *Okay, not a bad class to be in. But when did she register for this one? Why was everything so foggy in her brain? And she'd made a different set of choices ... or ... had she?*

"Yes, Echo," he said, in what sounded like an Irish accent. *Or Scottish?* She could never tell.

Once, in grade school, they had this foreign kid that was in her fourth- and fifth-grade classes. She thought he was British for two years and it wasn't until his last day at the school, in the fifth grade, when his family was moving back home to Australia, that she realized his nationality.

"It's an astute observation," the professor continued. "What's remarkable, though, is its ability to weave the narrative together."

"Yes, and? Sir?"

"Please, Echo, don't call me sir. And yes, we are discussing the peculiar properties of a *yes/and* mindset. Carol Dweck writes about it but she calls it something different. Can anybody tell me?"

A few people rush to their devices to look it up, but the professor cuts them off. "No cheating; it's okay, guys and gals, if you don't know something. It's additionally okay if you learn it from a human in person instead of one hiding in the Internet."

Laughter from the class ensued. "Growth mindset," Echo said.

"Right, Echo, thanks again. Its opposite is a fixed mindset, everyone," the professor said.

Another hand goes up at the same time Echo's hand does. It's that of a moppy-haired, muscly guy. He sounds British, so she assumes he's Australian. She notices he looks an awful lot like the kid from fourth and fifth grade. The professor calls on him.

The Aussie says, "I think it's an interesting correlation between a fixed mindset and the word fix."

"How do you mean?" Echo asks.

"Well, the word fix implies you think the something is broken. It just makes me wonder if the people with fixed mindsets or those in an *either/or* space see the world as black and white because they see it as a bit broken. Maybe it's what makes them think they need to have an answer, that they need to *fix* it."

The professor breaks into a broad smile, similar to Echo's, and says, "Ari, well said, and I noted you didn't pull out your phone a moment ago when you didn't know the answer."

"If you can sit and be uncomfortable until you're comfortable, you can learn a lot," Ari said, then turned to Echo, commenting, "And yes, I'm the kid from fourth and fifth grade, Echo, wake up!"

BANG! BANG! BANG!

Her boyfriend jolted Echo awake.

She turned on the car engine and opened the window. He stared at her, before asking, "What are you doing?"

She shrugged.

"Come on inside."

She shrugged.

"You're not still mad because I didn't bring your lame-ass clothes up to the theater, are you?"

She shook her head. She pursed her lips. She had some thinking to do. She had dreams that she was out of touch with — she had wanted to go to university and study strategic design, like designing whole ecosystems.

"Well, are you coming in or not? It's cold out here and I didn't come all the way out here just to stand here like an idiot."

Well, that's just your default mode, she thought. What she actually said was, "I'll be in in a little bit."

"Well, it's dumb not to at least have your heater on. So, leave the car running, I guess. Goodnight."

He walked off and she watched him go. She looked up at the dreamcatcher again. She wanted to go back to that reality, not this one. She didn't like what she was living. She didn't like not feeling like the hero of her own story.

The first step of the dreamcatcher asks simply:

who is the hero of your story?

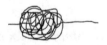

Echo waited a few moments until the duplex went dark. She turned the heater on and locked the car doors. She tapped the dreamcatcher and didn't feel anything this time. *No! She liked the person she was in the dream! Not this person! NO!*

Fearful, she tapped the dreamcatcher again. Nothing, once more. She watched it sway. She was oddly angry now. She was so rarely angry. But she was, she was angry. She ripped it down from the rearview and looked at it closely. *It was supposed to fix her problems, fix her ...!*

Wait.

Fix ...

Like she's broken. Like she's an *either/or. Damn ... that's easy to do*, she thought.

She took a deep breath, held the dreamcatcher to her heart until she could recognize her heartbeat, then laid her seat back and closed her eyes.

Yes, that's an easy trap to fall into and ...

As she accepted herself, she drifted again.

The second step of the dreamcatcher is to:
accept the hero and begin observing in a *yes/and*
to note what *they* feel and what *you* feel, then find
the connection between you and the hero
(even if it's you).

In a nutshell, this is empathizing

Echo was now walking into an office.

She stopped as she saw herself in the reflection of
the clean glass office window right before she
walked in. She was in "performance" clothes she
couldn't currently afford. *She looked damned good*, if
Echo had to say so herself. She stepped into the
office and looked over. Someone was talking to
her.

She saw a secretary, a young man in his mid-20s.
He showed her into a room that contained a large
white board. It had a white board table, too. In
fact, the whole room was covered in white

boards, with a few stacks of post-it notes on the table in front of her. She liked their colors.

But there was SWOT analyses everywhere on all kinds of topics but with similar themes.

side note:

"swot" means

strengths

weaknesses

opportunities

and threats

What is she supposed to do in here? Echo wondered.

She studied the boards. She noticed loads and loads of problem-solving. It seemed that each person had been attempting to assess the same thing. They were diagnosing a company problem. She studied each analysis, and most of them said something similar. *What a yawn-fest.* She sat down and waited. She was uncomfortable, but she was comfortable waiting for the next direction to appear. She sat in the ambiguity; she knew enough to know that patience is itself an action. A man walked in wearing a fashionable suit and no tie. She knew that moppy hair. When he spoke, she placed his Australian accent immediately. *She was getting better at this identifying dialect thing; see … a growth mindset can learn!*

"It's great to have you here, Echo. Please don't get up. We're not so formal here. Despite my suit. Truth is, I don't wear one very often," he said, grinning. "I knew you'd be here today. You look great, by the way."

Echo smiled. "Well, it looks nice, Ari. How can I be helpful to you?"

"Well, that's a great start. You're the first candidate we've had in three days that's asked how you can help us," Ari said, making some notes.

This is a job interview, Echo realized all at once.

"Excellent!" she said, maybe a little too enthusiastically.

If so, Ari didn't seem to notice or mind. He continued, "So, we have a problem. It's a big one.

And we'd be thrilled if you could help us solve it."

"Okay," Echo said, "my pleasure. You know I'd love to help if I can, Ari. I'd love to learn more about your problem."

Ari smiled and wrote something down. "The company is currently not profitable," he told Echo.

Ari seemed to wait a moment to see what Echo would do. She just sat and listened intently. She seemed to be empathizing. Ari wrote something else down and continued, "Well, it's not making money. We need to cut our workforce."

Ari paused again and studied her intently. She still didn't move. He went on, "The lay-offs are going to go badly, and we anticipate a rather large class action lawsuit, and so we need to plan for the inevitable. Will you help?"

Again, Ari hesitated as if waiting for Echo to do something. Surprising herself, as she always seemed to inside her dreams, Echo chimed in easily and without restraint, "May I ask you some questions, Ari?"

"Yes, of course," he replied.

"I think you mean *yes, and* of course," she thought and then said aloud.

He laughed. She did, too, as she grabbed five post-it notes.

Echo asked, "Ari, if your company is losing money, that must be a pretty scary thing, huh?"

Ari played along. "Yes, it's terrible. It's like being on the *Titanic*, Echo. You're walking down the hallways and noticing people everywhere that probably aren't going to be here much longer. Hell, you might even be one of them."

"May I ask you why they won't be here?"

"Because the company isn't making enough money to keep them on."

"Why?" Echo asked.

"They aren't hitting their quotas."

"And why is that? What's your take?" Echo asked.

"They don't have the product they need."

"Why?"

"We can't keep up with the demand."

The two of them sat there in the silent aftermath of having gone down the rabbit hole.

side note:

sakichi toyoda,

founder of toyota

industries which

made looms

is credited

with developing the

5 whys protocol

in the 1920s

The third step of the dreamcatcher is a modification of Sakichi Toyoda's 5-Why protocol we call *Chasing the Rabbit*.

What seems like a simple children's game gets us to root systems extremely swiftly. Here we go one step beyond empathy. But because we aren't using the 5-Whys in a typical manner, for problem-solving, we are chasing emotions through empathizing while attempting to deeply understand our hero. We call this process *Chasing the Rabbit*. It's like going down the rabbit hole in *Alice's Adventures in Wonderland*.

We know who our hero is … us or someone else … we've made observations on/about/around them and now we begin to chase their feelings down the rabbit hole in order to connect more.

let the whys take you to what and for whom we are really solving for in our work

"So, what are you saying, Echo?" Ari asked.

"I'm only clarifying right now, not asking or asserting anything. But am I hearing you say that you need to lay people off because you can't meet the demand of your customer base?" Echo asked.

"Well, it's not that simple, but yes, kind of …" Ari said tentatively; this was sailing into unchartered waters for him.

"So, right now, all of these SWOT analyses are designing for laying people off, or maybe with the aim of trying to become profitable?" Echo asked.

"Yes, Echo, so what would you recommend?" Ari queried in return.

"It's too early for me to recommend anything yet. I'm really just listening right now. That's what the dreamcatcher is all about, Ari. We need to make some discoveries as to what the real dreams are here. Because I'm guessing they weren't the prospect of laying people off," Echo observed.

"True story," Ari said.

Echo went on, "For now, I'd love to just observe what we've discovered so far, let's call it the shape of things. This is the narrative as it stands: you have a business that is succeeding. You have a great product and customers want it. So much so that you can't keep up with demand. So, your profits in the short-term are suffering. Yes, you need to make more money and ... yes, and ..."

"I'm listening," Ari said.

"... and you need more people in product development and in sales, not less. Once you have the ability to meet the demand, your cash flow drainage will cease and, in fact, reverse. Ari, you don't have a disaster. You have a success disaster."

"A success disaster? I love that term, Echo."

"Ari, your question is currently, 'How might we lay off people and stop the loss of money?' Correct?" she asked.

"Pretty much," he acceded.

"Well, inside that is one pretty big core assumption," she stated.

"And how'd you see that?" Ari asked.

"The dreamcatcher tells us. Right now, we've uncovered that your customers are not the hero of your story. You can always tell the hero because it's the person or entity you think you're solving for and, in this case, you've stated from the get-go that you are solving for your company. Yes?"

"Sure, I guess so," Ari said.

"And that means then that your hero is not who, Ari?" Echo questioned.

Ari shrugged.

"Who is giving you the success disaster?"

"The customer."

"Exactly. But you're solving for the company and not the customers, which means that you're asking completely different questions than you otherwise would. The 5 Whys revealed the core assumptions, and your initial line of questioning, plus my observations, showed me that you believed the customers' journeys to be a secondary storyline to that of the provider of the services, i.e. your company," Echo concluded, before taking a breath.

"Echo, where have you been all my life?" Ari asked, smiling. "You called this shaping earlier? What did that mean?"

She said, "It's a way of collating information and finding patterns and then reshaping, retrofitting, or re-story'ing it. For instance, you believe you need to lay off people to stop the loss of money? You might consider *shaping* that into, 'How might we stop losing money?' Because that could open up a host of brand-new questions, which means a bunch of fresh, innovative answers."

Ari sat grinning at his former classmate. He set his pen down, and said, "Echo, would you like a job?"

Echo woke to a phone call. She couldn't find her phone and so she missed it. She'd slept in her car all night long. She noted her car was running on empty. Her boyfriend's truck was gone.

She wanted desperately to make a change. Was she the hero of her own story? Had she given someone else that role? She knew the answer. She needed to run the dreamcatcher on herself. And she would, too, tonight.

Her phone rang again. She chased the ringing and found the device. It was Fingernail Pete. She was late for today's double at the Waffle House.

At least she was still wearing her uniform.

Later that night, after her shift, Echo stopped at Walmart and picked up post-its, markers, and a few white boards. She got home and drew a dreamcatcher-like shape. *It sucked*, she thought. Of course, her boyfriend got home and saw it. The duplex looked like chaos. He wasn't happy. But, then again, when was he ever? She was excited. She was becoming the hero of her own story. She decided she wanted to be a business designer and she told him so.

"Designer?" he snorted, "Echo, you couldn't design your way out of a paper bag."

She showed him part of the dreamcatcher exercise, the core of it, before it branched out into more and more whys. She wanted to show him how it kept going until it dug into her deeper quests.

She waited for him to take it in, before he asked, "Why does it say single and freedom? What am I looking at here, Echo?"

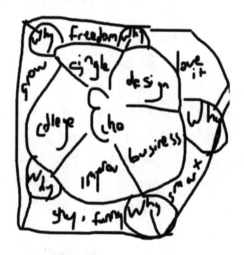

"My dreams," she said.

"What am I supposed to do with those?" he asked.

"In this story, the princess saves herself."

"And what does that mean?" he scowled.

"I'm leaving you," she said, with a forward heart.

As she left, she heard him echoing her words.

2.

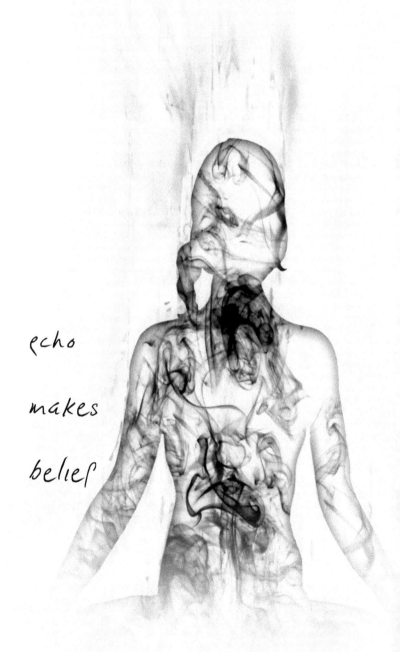

echo

makes

belief

an applicable
quote:

"we create our own life, and we
create it by our thinking feeling
patterns in our belief system."

louise hay

2.

Echo discovered she was the heroine of her own story, or the user of her own journey, or the audience member for whom she was solving. Further, she uncovered she hadn't been doing much solving for said audience member, user, or heroine. She'd been so misapplying her empathy that she was constantly solving problems for the people around her without giving herself the same attention. She used the dreamcatcher exercise, or the first step of the design thinking process, with a twist or two, in hopes of figuring out a way to do just that.

She discovered her pain points and why they were there. By uncovering how to use the modified 5-Why protocol, she went down the rabbit hole and discovered some painful and magical truths. She found that her life needed a redesign. She was so busy asking the wrong questions, the wrong, 'How might we _____?"

Her research could have just as easily been about someone else; she could have easily used the dreamcatcher on a client, like she did in the scenario with Ari after college. But allowing herself to ask what she wants, and *then* chasing it with whys until she is laid vulnerably bare, will take her to the truest places to build from for the longer term.

For instance, she discerned that she wanted to study business and design. She asked 'why business?' and realized she loved ways to use her brain, to stay sharp. She chose design because she loved it. But if she pressed in, she could have asked more whys. *Why do you love design?* "It's a way to contribute to society but still be creative," she may say. You can take the dreamcatcher and find patterns in the observations Echo made about areas that seemed important to her:

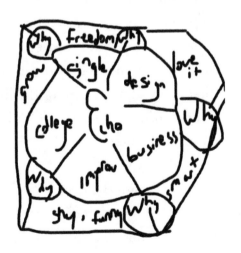

Digging into more *whys* reveals that Echo loves business and design because she wants to contribute. Her desire for college and improv both show us that she yearns to grow, learn, and isn't afraid to push herself with a challenge or two. She wrote down as her fifth observation, "single."

When she asked *why*, she got to freedom. Freedom also may be at the core of her desire to be smart, successful, to keep growing, and to help others. If that's the case, we would be in an interesting place to create inside because now we are getting into her core values.

If she yearns for freedom, she would never have been able to attain it in such a demanding or controlling dynamic. If she yearns for freedom, she can't remain stuck behind the veil of the painfully shy. If freedom is a driver for her, it will mean that she will need a lot of flexibility, autonomy, and continual co-creation in her plan or strategy for what's next.

Basically, Echo, through the dreamcatching exercise, has created her own character to use a storytelling term, or persona to use a design thinking term. She's empathized with her heroine and found that many changes will be needed in order to shift her heroine's reality. The next phase of Echo's journey will be in uncovering, discovering, or even creating the plot for her character, or the design for her persona. But she'll need something before she can move into that ideating place, the place of imagination and possible reality building. In both cases, she'll need a way in which the heroine sees the world.

In design thinking, it's called constructing a point of view. In storytelling, it's called creating your character's worldview. But, to do that in either framework, we will use an exercise from the belief-system building portion of the narrative design framework. It works because in both cases, it's the filters through which the practitioner will begin moving out of empathy and into re-framing (in design thinking) or using the re-story process (storytelling).

We've found some assumptions that Echo was making, but in order to shift her world enough to have a different view into it, she will have to discover them for herself. Especially now that we know she values independence so much. She may not even take advice from us right now.

The belief building exercise has its origins back in Konstantin Stanislavski's invention of the system for "method" acting. We've all heard the horror stories of actors going "too method." Let's hope we don't or that Echo doesn't. But there's an epic and life-changing tool buried in Konnie's work called the, "Magic If."[11] In this next piece of her story, she'll need to make some decisions based on her findings. She will have to face the assumptions she's been making and decide if they are solving for the right problems or not. And once she makes those decisions, she'll learn to employ the *Magic If*.

She already made one big change at the end of the last chapter. I think I can safely say it's one we'd have counseled her to make, given the opportunity. That fellow has some aggressive growing to do. Echo will also discover that once one moves out of the empathizing space and gets to patterning and point of view construction, we reach what storytellers call the point of no return.[vi] There's no coming back from realizing that you have been living and solving for lies, I'm sorry, I mean assumptions … or do I …?

---

[11] Stanislavski, K. (1989). *Stanislavski: An Actor Prepares*. New York: Theatre Arts Routledge.

Fingernail Pete still wouldn't look at her ass.

side note:

#win

The joy that this brought Echo was palpable.

tip:

if you

seek the end

of objectifying ...

humanize.

Echo couldn't help but notice that by her being all-too-human with F. Pete, she couldn't help but leave objectification. He definitely saw her as just another human now. She could always be grateful to "he-who-shall-not-be-named" for that at the very least. After all, it was his hatred of whispered frequencies that set the whole chain reaction off in the first place.

She poured black-rimmed coffee at table eight. Today was her first day of her next journey. It was also her last day at the Waffle House. She'd be okay if she never smelled like high-fructose corn syrup with maple flavoring ever again. *Why did I ever think that was maple syrup?* she wondered.

She looked up at the clock on the wall instead of the one on her phone. Her phone was not very popular these days. Echo had alienated all of her old friends, this guy had been *that* kind of a relationship, and she'd had precious few to begin with anyway. To be honest, her natural proclivity to introversion was really enjoying the silence.

The break-up could have gone better. But she chalked it up to having to have the hard conversations that leadership requires. She was planning to be a leader of designers. Her dreamcatcher revealed to her just how far she'd gone astray from her heart, from her dreams.

It turned out, not far. *Maybe it's never really as far as we think*, she thought, as she brought out the waffles and eggs over easy to some college kids.

I'll be one of you soon, she noted, as she dropped off the food and fielded the quest for extra butter — well margarine, not butter.

Echo was a butter kind of girl. She must have been making a face when she returned to the table and set the "butter" down.

One of the guys, a kid with a western beard, wide open in large spaces, asked, "Why the face? Something wrong with the butter?"

"No, I can honestly say there is nothing wrong with the butter."

He seemed pacified.

She went on, "This, however, is in fact a bunch of hydrogenated and genetically modified oils blended together into a frenzied state."

"Damn," he said, "you sound like my mom. You don't look like her, though. What are you doing when you get off work?"

"That's a great question. I'm going to build myself a point of view."

"A what?"

A throat could be heard being cleared over Echo's shoulder.

The young man with the crop-circle beard leaned back to see who it was that had tried to get their attention. Echo knew, she could smell the Band-Aids. F. Pete always seemed to smell like fresh Band-Aids.

side note:

the smell of

bandaids (also

sharpies, and

scotch whisky)

comes from cresols,

a certain kind of chemical

often used to dissolve

other chemicals

She looked askance at F. Pete. She'd taken to calling him "F. Pete" in her mind instead of Fingernail Pete. She thought it fitting given her early retirement from the house of Americanized waffles. She'd heard that in other countries, say Belgium for instance, waffles are used in savory meals. Her sister had dated someone from the deep south that loved chicken and waffles, but in her earnest youth and with the fixed mindset, she thought that absurd. She was rethinking so much. Since the dreamcatcher experience, which she couldn't tell anyone about, she'd been gobbling up everything she could on design thinking. She recently read a book called *The Design Way*.[12] It argued that humans didn't discover fire, but rather they designed it. She'd found the book serendipitously, at the sidewalk sale at the local bookstore.

She thought it fascinating that it showed up right after she became clear on where she wanted to go and what she wanted to do. She'd also been watching TED talks voraciously. Okay, so she was still using her phone. She had watched

---

[12] Nelson, H. G., & Stolterman, E. (2014). *The Design Way: Intentional Change in an Unpredictable World*. Cambridge, MA: The MIT Press.

Simon Sinek's *Start With Why* probably four times in the last two days. *Had it only been two days since she asked her ex to move out?* It was her duplex. She was the name on the lease. *He should be out by the time my shift is over.* As the thought washed over her, she smiled broadly. Another clearing of the throat. *F. Pete.* She turned to her manager. "How is everything at your table, gentlemen?" he asked. "I noticed that Echo here was spending a little extra time. Is there something wrong?"

The other young men at the table shook their heads no, clearly not wanting the interruption to their hang time. But another said, "Actually, sir"—he read Fingernail Pete's name tag— "Peter, I'm concerned about quality."

"Q-qu-qu-ality?" F. Pete stuttered. He always did when nervous about a potential corporate email. Echo glanced up at F. Pete's eyes and noticed that they were dilating, *a sign of stress.*

"Yes, Pete, quality. You see I've been made acutely aware that this so-called 'butter' is in fact not even high-quality margarine, if such a thing is more than an oxymoron. Could I please get some real butter for my waffle? That's what I was asking"—he looked right at Echo—"Echo."

"I s-s-see." Pete went to bite his nails.

Whenever Fingernail Pete stuttered, Echo's empathy was triggered. She couldn't let this guy make F. Pete's day miserable even if he was trying to have his *Good Will Hunting* moment. And not just because his beard was shit, but because for all of Pete's faults, he'd mostly been kind to Echo.

Also, because this guy was using someone else's hurt feelings to make her feel better and she had this hunch that you could make someone feel better without stealing those feelings from someone else.

The other guys at the table fought back a chuckle at Pete's stutter. Echo formed a point of view. "Peter, thank you for making certain that these gentlemen have what they need. That's a kind and thoughtful gesture. I'll go get their butter for them from the back," Echo said, and walked off quickly. Peter followed her. There was laughter at the table behind him.

Pete approached Echo in the break area by his office, which was really a storage closet in the back of house. "Echo, what was that, we don't have any real butter. This is an email for sure and I need this job. I can't have another one. I've been warned."

Echo dug around in the employee fridge. She looked up at Pete. "Didn't that new girl come in with a Starbucks bagel, earlier?"

Pete nodded; he looked suddenly embarrassed. "I saw her put the rest of it in here and I'm pretty sure she didn't use her butters."

It dawned on Pete what Echo was going for and he suddenly darted into the storage closet with a desk. He returned triumphantly with the bag from Starbucks.

"You ate after the new girl, didn't you, Pete?"

Pete chuckled as his blush warred with his excitement over the problem-solve. Echo saw him for the first time. Yes, he was definitely someone that was always playing *Magic: The Gathering* with the people in his life. *But aren't we all in our own ways?* she thought. How many times had she seen someone she knew in public and ducked around the corner, not because she didn't like them, but because she was enjoying the illusion she was in her own world?

She smiled at Peter.

"Peter, do you like 'Pete'?"

"Either is fine, but if I were to ch-choose, I'd say that I prefer Peter. Like Peter Jackson."[13]

"Like Peter Jackson," Echo said, nodding.

"Hey, you echoed me, Echo," he said, giving a genuine laugh. Echo tensed but listened. It was nowhere near an acerbic laugh. It was the kind of laugh a person enjoying a moment makes. She decided she would enjoy it, too.

"The butter," she reminded him.

He enthusiastically dug into the bag and found one golden pat of salted Kerrygold butter. Echo preferred the unsalted herself. It was cultured butter and she'd read that cultured butter's enzymes helped you digest everything better.

---

[13] Peter Jackson co-wrote the screenplays for and directed the J. R. R Tolkien epic trilogies of *The Hobbit* and *The Lord of the Rings*.

"There are usually two," she said.

Peter, *like Peter Jackson*, smiled sheepishly. *A sheep! That's what Peter, like Peter Jackson, reminds me of! I love sheep!* Echo smiled. *Ah, he even bleats.* Now she was permanently endeared. She couldn't believe that in only the last moments of her working at the Waffle House did she realize she could be friends with her manager.

What other things in life had she missed before she had her empathy back again to spend on other things and people?

"One's fine," Echo said.

He tried to hand it to her but she shook her head. "Please, Peter (*like Peter Jackson*, she thought), will you take it to their table. I'm afraid the guy that put you down was trying to hit on me by hurting your feelings. I don't really want to see him again."

"That makes sense, Echo. I'm sorry you had to feel uncomfortable. Or if you ever did while working for me here at the Waffle House," Peter said, and went to deliver the butter.

Echo stood in her empathy and couldn't believe what had just happened. She thought about the point of view she was developing. It was vague. In *The Design Way* they talked about how design is different from the arts and sciences in that it is inherently "others-focused," because it always exists in some kind of spoken or unspoken service relationship.

She wanted more and more to serve others ... *just not at the Waffle House*. She knew she needed to go back to school. Peter returned and smiled.

"What are you smiling about?" Echo asked.

"I gave them the butter with your regrets."

"Say more," Echo was intrigued.

"I told them you were indisposed."
Peter was smirking, sheepishly.

"And maybe that I was laughing to help it come out?" They shared a laugh in what felt like a well-designed moment.

"Your time's up," Peter said, "so, where are you headed?"

"Back to school to study strategic design maybe."

"I have no idea what that is, but I'm certain you'll be great." Peter smiled and rubbed his hands on his pants. It's what he did when he didn't need to bite his nails.

"Have you thought about doing something else?"

"Sure, Echo, I'm at the Waffle House," he stated, more directly than anything she'd ever heard him say.

She nodded and took it in. "What's stopping you?"

Silence fell like snow in early spring, large flakes and slowly, quietly.

"Me."

Echo took in the gift of his vulnerability. She moved to her bag in the corner of the break room. She rummaged and took out a worn book. She handed it over to Peter.

He looked down at it for a long time. He pulled out a pen. He handed her the pen and the book, asking, "Would you sign it?"

She took them both and thought for a moment, before writing: *"Humans didn't discover fire, they designed it.*

"Design yours, Peter 'Jackson.' Your new friend, Echo." She handed the book back to Peter.

"I wish I had something for you, Echo," he said.

She was thoughtful for a moment and then asked, "Can I have the apron and waitress outfit?"

Echo is developing her point of view. But she's doing it through the empathy learnings about herself. She's identified her user as herself. But now, as she gains understanding and the empathy she's experiencing builds bridges between her and others like her, she's realizing that what she's doing to serve herself (because that's her user) has much broader applications. Her point of view is emerging, but right now, she doesn't know exactly how to engage it. She doesn't yet have a tool to pull it out of the world of mental processing. We have a tool for her, don't worry. It's easy to use and you can use it, too. For this we are going back to the world of Echo and her improv troupe. They are in the middle of a performance. They are playing a game inspired by the work of ol' Stanislavski. So, let's connect with them, their audience, our Echo, and this method to the madness.

There are loads of ways to frame design after you've done your research and found patterns and insights. Keep in mind, this is only one. (A fun one — but still only one.)

Echo stands in her waitress outfit on the edge of the stage as Big Mike speaks to the audience, a full house of energized people. "So, that was a lot of fun. You don't always get to see that on a random Saturday night. What were some of your favorite bits?"

"The waitress in the bathroom!" a woman yelled.

The crowd agreed and cheered loudly. Big Mike smiled. "Well, don't try that at home. She isn't an actual waitress, she only plays one on stage."
Cue laughter.

"No other bits? Okay, well, that's a good start. Nowhere near the participation I need. It's like you guys thought I said get out and vote."
More laughter.

"Okay, fine. What if I give you stickers? That's really what gets people to vote, isn't it?"
Cheers.

"I didn't say what they were. They are Dicks."
Bursts of Laughter.

"Jade, Echo, Johnson … and … and …" Mike delays on purpose. They pick up on "Johnson."

Continued laughter from the audience. In the meantime, full of enthusiasm, Jade and Echo grab a page of stickers from Mike and head out among the audience. Eric Johnson walks up to take a page of stickers from Big Mike.

He leans into Mike's mic and with perfect timing Mike tilts the hand-held mic in his direction. "Johnson, Eric Johnson," Eric says, with all the spirit of James Bond that he can muster. Laughter ensues as Johnson takes his place in a corner of the room around the audience.

"… and Jimmy."

Further laughter as a very short man, presumably Jimmy, jogs up and grabs the rest of the stickers from Big Mike.

"Okay, now that we've primed the pump, let's talk voting. We have already voted for the waitress. Who said that?"

A hand shoots up in the audience and Jade runs over with a sticker. She hands it to the woman. The woman looks at it and makes a face. Big Mike milks it, asking, "Is it or is it not a Dick?"

Jade holds a hand-held mic to the woman, who responds, "It is, technically, yes. But …"

"No, no butts on stickers, ma'am, that's just offensive."

Laughter.

"Who's next? We have the waitress. Who else from tonight's show?"

"The farm animal!" someone yells. Eric Johnson and Jimmy both make a run for them and neither yield. They play up a collision as they reach the man's table. They both hand him a sticker at virtually the same time.

"They've been competing all night," Big Mike says, "it's not you, it's them."

"What do I do?" the man says.

"Ah, the human dilemma," Big Mike counters, "I suggest you take both for the farm animal selection you made."

Cheeky guffaws all around. The man, blushing, takes the stickers. He looks at them and laughs, then shows them to the people on his table, who also chuckle.

"If you haven't figured it out by now, the stickers are pictures of former President of the United States, Tricky Dicky Nixon."

The people who didn't already know gasped "Oh!" and "Ah!"

"What? Oh, did you think … oh, my goodness," Big Mike admonishes the audience. "Get out of here with your dirty minds."

The audience erupts again, then the other four participants, characters from earlier on in the show, are chosen in quick succession. The rest of the stickers are placed on each table.

"The game we are playing is called 'If, Then, But …' and everyone with a sticker can help write the storyline. We are going to build a world and if you have a sticker on you can help." People pass around more stickers. "I'm ashamed of where your minds went," Mike says.

"If, Then, But," is a game developed by *storylab*[14] and is an epic way to build the rules of your design constraints[vii] or rules of world.[viii] Plus, it can be wicked fun.

In this case Big Mike and, by proxy, Echo, will use this game to establish the rules of world for which the characters will all play in. Note carefully, because they will engage the first stage of the design process in order to build the second and create a design.

Creating the design will be the subject of the improvisational comedy game. But, for our purposes, it makes a pretty swell analogy.

Before we cut back to their game in process, let's dissect the process:

1) Start with a persona/character
   a. Ask what this character was doing five minutes before now and is planning to do five minutes after he/she leaves us

[14] *storylab* is the design lab dedicated to the power of story in the world. Discover more of their exercises at storylab.tv

b. What do they hate that they are afraid to tell anyone?

c. What do they love that no one knows about?

2) Craft with the "Magic If"

a. Lay out the structure of where each person has come from and where they are going, highlighting that we don't know what's about to happen to them here and now.

b. Look for patterns in the answers — draw correlations from seemingly unrelated pieces, dig abnormally deep, and reach for assumptions.

c. Ask "If" about the combined answers from question one.

d. Ask "Then" about the combined answers with the goal of discovering their hidden intentions or designs on life.

3) Limit with a big but

a. Create a constraint by discovering the reason they aren't doing the thing they want to do.

b. Develop a point of view on why they are letting that limit them.

c. Then your design identifies the jam and creates the fix.

For example: "*If* our waitress just came from the DENTIST and is on her way to PLANT TOMATOES BEFORE THE IMPENDING FROST and she secretly hates THE SMELL OF CRESOLS (LIKE IN BAND-AIDS AND SCOTCH WHISKY) and she loves when other people say the word HEY, BECAUSE IT REMINDS HER OF COMMUNITY FARMS, *Then* she really wants to be a farmer (clue: planting and the word "hey") because she hates the smell of medicines (clue: read into the smell of cresols). But even though she wants to be a farmer, she can't because she has dental problems and wouldn't be able to afford it by growing tomatoes and so she has to stay in the city and work.

Her Jam:
She's working just to pay the doctor.

Her Fix:
Start paying the farmer instead of the doctor.

Now on stage it plays out as chaos. But safely directed chaos as all good creativity should be. The key is secrecy. No one knows what the storylines selected by the audience are or the scenarios that the characters will find themselves in. Let's head back.

People are guffawing as Johnson chases Jimmy off stage, braying like a donkey.

Big Mike is on the mic. "Okay, okay, okay! That's what happens in 'If, Then … But …' when a wrestler that's always wanted to best a wild animal sees a donkey dancing in the fields as it's always wanted to …"

The laughter calms and he reads from his cards, "Our next scenario is 'end of the world, with a waitress that wants to be a designer on HGTV!" Echo runs out to cheers and whistles. She takes a bow.

Big Mike carries on, "Samson from the bible, who wants to be in the New Testament instead of the Old Testament … who writes this stuff … oh, that's right … we all did … you weirdos, oh, and that's me, wait, where are my cheers?"

People cheer and he continues half-satisfied, "And a schoolteacher who dreams of being a storm chaser on a motorcycle with a sidecar." Mike shakes his head and tosses the card.

She had to slam her brakes on a bit in the driveway, causing the dreamcatcher to sway. She reached up and stopped its movement. "Oh no you don't, I've already learned my lesson." She turned the car engine off and let out a huge sigh. His truck was gone. No blue lights flickering violent video games in the duplex she pays for every month.

She briefly wondered where he was and then decided that wasn't an energy invested that she would get much return on. *Tonight was a blast.* When Big Mike, or Samson, brought that bridge down over them in a perfect shelter from the tornado they'd chased down on a motorcycle with one another … all she could say as the world was ending was that she hoped HGTV would get the video she'd been taking of their new design show, "Helping people make a change using spiritual quest design."

It's funny, because that's kind of what I'm actually on, she thought. *I wonder if "If, Then, But ..." would help me form my point of view?*

She went inside to find out.

It was time to create the rules of her world.

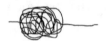

When you set out to design the rules of the narrative that you'll be creating inside, there are a few key things to remember.

One, the process is only that, a process. This means that you can't f_*k it up. In fact, how would you create differently, or even live differently, if you knew that there was no messing up and only process. In many ways, that's the fundamental key to the narrative design mindset: the process or journey is the actual destination. Perfectionism is already dead; our mindset just hasn't caught up as a society. We still shoot for the ideal. Which is doubly hard for idealists like me (and maybe you), but we must fundamentally accept that the ideal is a moving target. And that will small change will make us like the kind of person comfortable in the process. Processes are mindset makers and ego takers. Destinations are for egos.

Two, just because you're iterative,[ix] doesn't mean you don't rock star some excellence. As Master Yoda said, "Do or do not, there is no try." There's no room for "b-games" rather than "a-games" in a society that's ever-changing and rapidly so. This may sound like a lot of pressure and it is, but it's not any more so than what we've been misplacing on ourselves in a non-generative and destructive manner in the hidden gem of perfectionism. The difference here is you are in an exchange with another, be it an audience, users, customers, or even — as we see with Echo — yourself and the immediate world around you.

Three, remember it's always a human exchange and that will keep you in empathy, in excellence, and in iteration. There's a saying in counselling (I've ghostwritten books for counselors): *people marry a person and divorce a role.* What that means is that we fall in love inside an exchange with another human being, but we all too easily allow ourselves to begin identifying with the roles we play in coupledom. "I have to ask the wife," or "I'm not sure what the husband will think of that," are common phrases, but both denote identification with playing roles and all that comes with that. It's easy to dehumanize roles, like we saw with Echo and her "boss," F. Pete. However, when he became Peter, she wasn't talking to her boss anymore, she was having an exchange with another human being. The people involved in the machine made something human in the world, even a corporate one. As we are about to see, there are ways to do just this and again we will turn to storytelling as Echo runs into a wall.

Echo ran inside to the wall she had the dreamcatcher exercise on and tore it down. She needed the space. She was so inspired that she forgot to take a picture of it first. So, she plastered the extra-large 2'x2' post-it[15] back onto the wall and took a photo of it, then discarded it.

---

[15] These XXL post-it notes are unbelievably epic for the design thinking, storytelling, or narrative design process. (Also for love notes to someone or yourself … nothing says affirmation like four square feet of #LiveYourDeepestBliss)

She carefully drew another of the giant-sized post-its off of the large tablet and posted it up on the wall. She drew a triangle:

then:

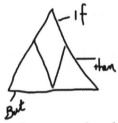

In her "If" column she wrote her love, design. Then added a "Then": school.

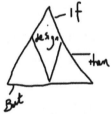

But, now she hit the wall. Because, in realizing to design systems in the way she wanted to Echo knew she would have to go back to school. So, she asked herself the third and most vital part in helping her dig down into her next constraint.

She asked herself why she doesn't do that already? What's been holding her back from living this or creating this dream?

Her answer surprised her and seemed on the surface like it shouldn't be a blockade to the future.

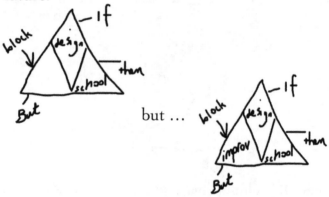

but …

Improv? She tossed her pen down and went to pee. She had to process this. That was unexpected. She remembered the dreamcatcher and its rabbit hole. She returned refreshed and dropped into a 5-Why protocol to better understand her user, herself.

I can't leave for design school because of improv. There are improv troupes everywhere. Right? So, what's the big deal?

Maybe the "whys" would tell her so she could build forward.

She took a photo of the 2x2 "If, Then, But" on the wall and then ripped it down. Next, she plastered a fresh 2x2 on the wall and then drew a dreamcatcher diagram; she wondered if it would work as well as an idea as it did as a persona—it was all still connected, so she hoped it would. She needed it to succeed. She yearned for a sincere point of view to create with for the foreseeable future.

It looked like this:

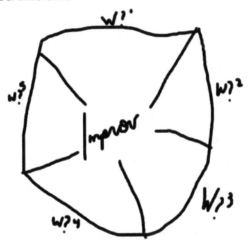

I.   Why? *I love it.*
II.   Why? *I feel freer there than anywhere.*
III.   Why? *I can be any me I dream up.*
IV.   Why? *I'm not afraid.*
V.   Why? *It's a safe place to fail.*

She contemplated returning to the dreamcatcher for her "If" of design and her "Then" of school. But she felt pretty clear about those and their whys. *Hey! I'm starting with "why" just like Simon Sinek[16] says to do! BOOM!* she thought. She hadn't read the book, but she'd watched the TED talk.[17] Then, she wondered if she should use it on her feeling. That would move it from the standard 5-Why Protocol to the dreamcatcher's rabbit hole. Because it's digging deeper and going into the emotions to really find the pain points of our user and in this case … Echo didn't know if she felt strong enough to do it by herself right now. *There's already so much change.*

But … it was time for a little couraging.[x] She took a picture and ripped the 2'x2' down. She put another up in its place and drew another dreamcatcher and wrote a statement at its center. Then, she drew the 5 Whys around it. She had started to hit a wall, when she'd discovered she wasn't leaving town because of the improv troupe. Now, it was time to rip off the Band-Aid.

---

[16] Sinek, S. (2013). *Start With Why: How Great Leaders Inspire Everyone to Take Action*. London: Portfolio/Penguin.
[17] www.TED.com puts out the greatest talks on the planet Earth.

As Echo was writing, she found herself tearful and couldn't have told you why. However, they were tears of gratitude waiting to fall from her eyes. She was listening deeper to her soul than she had in a very long time … maybe ever.

She asked:

1) Why? *I'm afraid.*
2) Why? *I will be found out.*
3) Why? *I am an impostor.*
4) Why? *I don't feel confident.*
5) Why? *I don't believe in myself.*

Echo sunk into her flea-market-find leather club chair with a tear in the ottoman. She'd moved it over to the wall for more comfortable thinking. She closed her eyes and focused on her breath. It was hitting her; all the book reading, the waiting tables, the improv, was all there in place, serving her in order for her to learn to believe in herself. But now—now it was out in the open. Now the energy investment and why she was doing it were apparent. She was ready to design for her user. She had her point of view … *how did those "point of view" statements begin again? "How might we," that's right … So … how might I design a life that … no … too broad. Much bigger than a paper bag.*

Another gift he-who-shall-not-be-named left for Echo was that now she thought of her situation as a paper bag. He had said, "Echo, you couldn't design your way out of a paper bag." She'd taken it to heart and reframed it into a compliment because paper bags are really quite fragile. She'd since unwittingly taken to seeing this whole exercise as designing her way out of a paper bag. She went back to her design statement, her point of view, her rules of world.

How might I learn to … no. How might I believe in myself through … definitely not. How might I design my way out of a paper bag?

She laughed and stood up out of the chair. She ripped down the 2x2 and wrote on the wall with her marker:

echo designs her way out of a paper bag

There went the deposit. She stood back. It was meaningful to her and it was what she needed for her user. But she had a hunch that she would need it in design terms, too, at some point.

So, she wrote underneath it in square brackets:

[how might i gain creative confidence and

live my dreams sooner rather than later]

She liked that enough. Besides, it was in marker pen on the wall. She plopped back into the club chair and crashed into a deep sleep where she dreamed of a storm coming, a massive storm, and it seemed like it was coming from her and outside her at the same time. It was the end of the world … the world as she had known it, anyway.

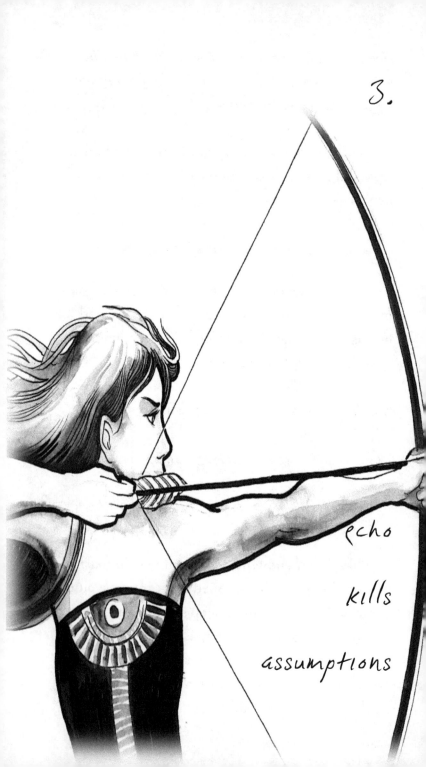

3.

echo

kills

assumptions

quotes

remain

thematic:

"vulnerability is the birthplace of

innovation, creativity, and change."

brene "badass" brown[18]

---

[18] Brené Brown is the author of several books and the research behind the "power of vulnerability" movement.

3.

I have this wicked-smart Harvard grad that I
was working with on a narrative design jam
sesh[19] for a client and she made a fascinating
statement about strategy. I'm a Parsons kid and
so I like Harvard kids because they were brought
up in a different culture to me. Working with
them is anthropological for me. She mentioned
that strategy is about what we say "no" to, not
about to what we say "yes." I thought about that
long and hard and had to agree. The amount of
times in my life I said "yes" when a "no" would
have been epically strategic are too many to
number. For instance, it would have been a
helpful mental model in high school come Sadie
Hawkins Day Dance. I said yes way too fast.
Fear sucks unless you're running from a
dinosaur, then fear rocks so hard.

Context is everything. Which was my second set
of thoughts after stewing about what a great
strategizer "no" can be for us. And yet, we sure
as heckfire don't hear the word "yes" often
enough. We've discussed this already, earlier in

---

[19] urban-nerd slang for "session."

the book, in the power of the "*yes/and*"
phenomena.

side note:

did you know that

the average toddler

hears the word

"no" on average 400

times a day and 10,000

times by the age of 6? [20]

So, while "no" may be great for strategy, it's shit
for creativity and a real deal-killer in ideation
sessions.[xi] To the Harvard lady's credit, when I
brought this topic back up, she agreed. She went
on to tell me a behavioral science story about a
brainstorming session she'd heard from the
horse's mouth. (I like horses more than many
people; this is not an offensive statement.)

---

[20] Dancy, R. B. (2012). *You Are Your Child's First Teacher:
Encouraging Your Child's Natural Development from Birth to Age Six.*
New York: Ten Speed Press.

The story goes that in a certain town in the north where it gets really very cold, a group of decision makers, scientists, and other persons were in a room together trying to solve the problem of power lines getting caked with ice. The ice was wreaking havoc on the power grid and contributing to serious blackouts. The facilitator, a behavioral scientist, stated that there was only one rule to their ideation or brainstorming session they were about to conduct. She stated, "There can be no bad ideas, meaning every idea is acceptable, we won't be shaming any kind of creativity here today, even if it sounds silly."

Everyone in the room seemed nervous because of this statement and more than one of them shot worried glances toward an eccentrically dressed gentleman sat in the corner eating a powdered sugar six-pack of mini donuts from the vending machine. He clearly chewed very well. His mastication rate was several bites down per mini donut. But he chewed with his mouth open, though how he managed to keep the smacking sound at bay was a mystery to all who stood next to him. He did, however, because of the openness of his mouth, and his rate of chew placed a fair amount of mini-donut dust on his considerable red beard.

The facilitator opened the session. The ideas started pouring forth.

"We could put space heaters at the base of poles."

"How about we bury them? It's healthier anyway."

"What if we used slightly less thick cables to make them warmer or changed out the cables with lighter and more conductive winter cables?"

The facilitator wrote and wrote on the white board. She was enjoying the speed at which the ideas were coming. And everyone was treating one another with respect and a real *yes/and* attitude. There was no wrong creativity. A throat cleared and then she heard a wrapper crinkle in only the way that cellophane can. She turned to the red-bearded man. He met her gaze and nodded. He raised his hand. The others ideating stopped cold in their tracks.

The whole energy of the room changed. The facilitator noted the dread. This piqued her curiosity. "Sir, you don't have to raise your hand. You can just blurt it out."

He left his hand up and in a fashion she couldn't distinguish between a too-much-powdered-sugar-in-the-throat cracking yell or a minor case of Asperger's, he blurted out, "bear!"

The whole room looked at the man. The facilitator was all set to write down the "no bad ideas" idea. She heard some murmurs from others; the room would sour if she didn't roll with it.

She uncapped her marker and wrote, "Bears!" as enthusiastically as the other ideas.

"Honey!" the man blurted.

"We cake the honey on the lines!" she wrote. No one else was participating, but the red-bearded man was on a roll, and he blurted out again, "Bears love honey, right?"

"Oh man, this is so easy. Get honey on the lines and the bears will follow. Their weight will displace the ice. It's simply physics."

One more blurt produced, "And biology! Because bears love honey and that fact is part of biology!"

Silence filled the room. The man had effectively tested everyone's willpower to say yes to every idea. The facilitator felt all eyes on her as she wrote with her back to them. She worked to get her smile under control and turned around to face them. "And how will we get the honey on the power lines?"

The man looked extremely puzzled and earnestly turned to his colleagues for support. Someone strong in empathy took charge, shouting, "Helicopters!"

The red-bearded man caught the vision. "Exactly! They drop it on the lines and boom! Bears!"

The ideation session continued until a hundred ideas had been generated. But do you know which idea they settled on?

Helicopters.

If helicopters flew close enough to the power lines, their blowback from the blades in motion decimated the ice that had gathered on the lines. No bears or honey, but effective and the helicopters would have never made an appearance if the idea had been laughed off.

How might I ... how might I ...?

Echo was looking online at the library. The computer in the house had been Mr. *Call of Duty*'s. She loved libraries anyway. She was torn between using the money she'd saved to get a new job or putting it towardmoving and going to a school somewhere that she'd yet to gain acceptance into.

She sighed and closed the laptop she'd just checked out from the computer vending machine with her library card. She loved, deeply loved, innovations like this; it gave her hope in humanity. She decided that she would go and browse the fiction area for a change. She'd been on such a non-fiction kick that she hadn't had the chance to read anything make-believe lately. She saw *The Alchemist*,[21] a favorite of hers that she'd read many times since it was assigned in eighth grade. Something like that would be good right now. She thumbed through a few books and then looked for indigenous authors. She saw *The Four Agreements*, and recognized it. She'd heard good things about it. But it was in that gray area between fiction and non-fiction. She wanted fiction. Something a little odd or obscure.

She found an author named Tse-Gi and picked up the book and looked through it. It was called *The Soul Traders*[22] She thumbed to a page on where a line caught her attention: "Decision is a murderer. It's why the Trader found it so hard to make one. To take one path was to kill the others. He knew that while decision may be a killer, it was also the most powerful force available to humans. He wondered where his fear was founded then? What comes before decision?" She closed the book and put it back. *Ugh. That was intense. But that's how I feel right now. Like I'm going to kill all other possibilities if I choose one path.*

---

[21] Coelho, P. (n.d.). *The Alchemist*. New York: HarperCollins.

[22] Tse-Gi (2018). *The Soul Traders*. Cambridge: White Bison.

She was grateful for improv rehearsal tonight. She'd often thought about looping them in, but why she felt safe in their presence was because they didn't really know her. And they may freak out if they knew they were losing the waitress … *if they were losing the waitress*. She had to find a way to implement her design. She had a point of view, a rule of world, but no world yet.

It was Big Mike who saw it first, it was always Big Mike who saw it first. *How did he always know?*

"I'm an empath,[xii] Echo. We empaths have to stick together. Don't look so surprised. You're not alone," Big Mike said.

"I feel alone lately," she said.

"What's the jam, maybe we can improv our way out of it tonight as the rehearsal?"

"Oh, G*d no! That's so intense, Mike," Echo said, surprised at her own emotional violence.

Jade walked up with Johnson, Eric Johnson, and Jimmy. Actors are drawn to drama like bears to honey on power line poles in the far north. They hovered like helicopters over power lines in winter.

"Did you know that improvisation was one of humanity's first forms of innovating problems, all kinds of problems?" Big Mike went on.

"That's ridiculous," Echo said.

"Jade? She's quite a nerd, listen up, Echo."

Echo looked over at Jade. Jade motioned for everyone to sit in a circle on the stage. This was normal for their rehearsals. They practiced lots of improvisational games this way.

Johnson, Eric Johnson went over and hit the stage lights, then turned the houselights off. It was just them now in a circle of light. *There's nothing quite like this*, Echo thought.

She looked over at Jade, who in typical Jade fashion turned it into a warm up. One of Echo's favorite things about the woman, and she knew very little about her, was that she could integrate storylines into scenes better than anyone Echo had ever met. Jade pulled a box over and started drumming on it. She stopped suddenly and pulled her colorful, gypsy-looking scarf over her head and suddenly she was drumming again, and she was a gypsy. Echo was transported immediately. She swayed to the beat that the gypsy played.

Jade stopped the drumming again quite suddenly and said in an old fortune-teller woman's voice, "Listen one, listen all, for the tale I tell shall soon enthrall …"

The drumming began again …

… And stopped. "The tale goes to a place told of in the cards … a kingdom with a lone storyteller, a bard …"

More drumming.

Jimmy and Johnson, Eric Johnson both got up to be the bard at the same time. After a scathing look from Jade at both, without her breaking her drumbeats, they both sat back down. She shook her head but didn't break character.

She nodded to Johnson, Eric Johnson and stopped drumming, and he got up swiftly, pulled his long hair back into a man bun, jutted his chin out proudly, and swept his hand across those gathered in a gesture of "hear ye, hear ye …"

"The bard knew the history of the king's delights, but he was also sad keeper of the king's many fights."

Drumming.

The bard mimicked seeing things he didn't want to see and then secretly kept the histories. Echo watched in amazement.

The drumming stopped once more.

"The king had a son, a princeling of spirits …"

The gypsy nodded to Jimmy. Jimmy stood and looked to be smiling way too much, and disingenuously at that. Big Mike stood, taking his cue to be the king.

"The king was blinded to the inner screams his people would make when interacting with the princeling."

She drummed and picked up the speed. The three actors interacted in a strange dance of emotions on stage together. It was mesmerizing in the shadows and light of the circle on the stage. Echo grinned from ear to ear, her troubles temporarily forgotten.

With the drumming stopping again, so too did the actors freeze.

The gypsy said, "The bard, being a goodly man of heart that's kind, knew there was no way a plain-speaking man could change the king's mind, and so devised a show, improvised in the great hall during a day of snow …"

She drummed and stopped. "All in the courts of the castle came, and the bard created a show about a prince insane."

The princeling on the stage became visibly upset. The bard looked nervous but kept acting it out. The king seemed entertained and the gypsy continued, "All the court saw it there but still the king could not see or else seemed he did not care. But now the bard and his players became the king and showed him to think he was exactly like the princeling."

"Like father like son, like apple like tree, like king like prince, like truth like me, unless one wakes one will not see!" the bard said.

The king looked flabbergasted and the princeling stood, bellowing, "This is an outrage! I am nothing like my father! I see him as insane! Do not compare me to him! You call yourself a bard and I say simpleton!"

The gypsy said, "The king's shock turned on his son and for the first time he saw his ..."

I was talking to someone last year that worked on Hillary Clinton's "I'm With Her" campaign.

It struck me as I spoke with her that she was still very much processing her hurt over the loss suffered in Hillary's camp, all those disavowed hopes and deeply held beliefs that it was time for a woman to be president. That's a certain storyline and she found herself in the opposite reality of the storyline she'd hoped to create. I won't rock politics here, but I will say I love women in leadership. I love what the research shows that, as a group, they do with power and even more what they do with their money. But I'm Cherokee and we are a matriarchal society. I told this to my new friend.

I then asked her what she was most surprised by in the whole endeavor. She grew quiet, then said, "I just didn't think, none of us thought, that he could actually win." I remembered back to something my new friend and fellow strategic designer had said earlier that evening, that, "You have to kill your assumptions."

Well, that was a pretty big-ass assumption.

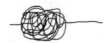

Echo looked at her troupe. They all looked at her back. Finally, Jade said, "Well? Echo?"

"What did he see?" Echo asked.

"On-his-son rhymes with …" Jimmy asked.

"On-his-son, on-his-son, on-his-son ..." Echo echoed, and then she jumped up to join them, shouting, "ASSUMPTION!"

Big Mike said, "So, can you see that improv and drama have been used to make people see things forever?"

"And this is WAY before cognitive behavioral therapy got involved," Jade said. "They've kind of co-opted the whole play and role-playing thing from those of us better trained for it."

"You don't sound bitter at all, Jade," Johnson, Eric Johnson said.

"Or before HBR started ranting about it, I remember that's why you sought out improv to begin with, Echo," Big Mike said.

"H-B-R?" Jimmy asked.

"Harvard Business Review," Jade said.

"Oh! That explains all the business books in your bag the day it spilled. You are one of those types," Jimmy said.

"What types? Don't make assumptions about me, Princeling!" Echo countered.

"Who's up for playing Amish Inquisition?"[23] asked Big Mike.

Everyone sat down to play except Echo, who still felt a little confused. She slowly started to sit and was redirected by Jade to sit in the middle.

"Don't we need a horse and buggy?" Echo said, as she dragged the black box Jade had drummed on into the center of the circle.

"Looks like you already have one," Jimmy said.

"I assumed it was just a chair," Echo said, smiling.

"You're already getting the idea," Jade said.

---

[23] *storylab* is the design lab dedicated to the power of story in the world. Discover more of their exercises at <u>storylab.tv</u>

Over twenty years ago, I read a small volume called *Let Your Life Speak*,[24] by Parker Palmer, an author who notably enjoyed getting old and never thought he would. This little volume is worth your time if you're looking for a fresh take on finding your vocation in life. Palmer spent a fair amount of time living with the Amish as an "English" man, which is what the Amish call outsiders, *the English*.

He had committed to them for a certain amount of time. He was studying and wanting to learn of their way of life. He received a call from a small but prestigious college that asked him to be their president. His time with the Amish wasn't yet up. Because he was uncertain about what he would do, even though he was heavily leaning toward taking the opportunity, he asked for the Amish right of elder council.

He sat before a group of elders in a barn and they asked him question after question. He wasn't allowed to say anything back or justify his case, only to observe his inner reaction. The questioning went on for a long time. Finally, one

---

[24] Palmer, P. J. (2000). *Let Your Life Speak: Listening for the Voice of Vocation*. San Francisco: Jossey-Bass.

elder, a man who'd not spoken the entire time, spoke up.

As he stroked his thick, gray beard, he said, "Now, Parker, you can speak to this. Thank you for listening to our questions. I have only one more and I want you to say what comes to mind without thinking too much about it."

Parker nodded.

The elder continued with his hand still petting his own beard, "What are you most excited about in getting this job as president of a prestigious college?"

Without thinking, Parker blurted out the first thing that came to mind, "I'll get to have my picture in the paper."

One by one the elders looked at Parker, nodded, and departed. The man who spoke last was also the last to leave. He turned from the door back to a stunned Parker, and asked, "Do you think there might be other ways to get your picture in the paper?" #Assumption #AmishForTheWin

Larry D. Hargrave, is a pre-eminent researcher on assumptions, specifically as it applies to two different arenas. He has a book coming out soon, called *Same, Not Same*,[25] in which he shares his monumental findings from forty-five years of research around what he calls the "assumption of similarities."

According to Hargrave's research, when we encounter someone new, our brains make one single narrative differentiation: *Are they like me or are they different from me?* This one assumption forms the basis of every interaction we have from that point forward, every belief we create about the other party, and each agreement or disagreement that follows. It should come as no surprise that if we assume we are similar, we are far more likely to accept him or her, and if we assume dissimilarity we are far more apt to judge the other person. Our tendency to assume is nothing new. But shockingly, we don't take much time to evaluate whether or not the foundations of our dreams, or our intentions, or our plans, whether professional or personal, are grounded in truth or the dare to assume.

---

[25] Hargrave, Larry D. (2020). *Same, Not Same: How One Assumption Changes Everything*. Los Angeles: storylab® books.

The group has been grilling Echo for at least twenty minutes. They make statement after statement, all based in assumptions or—in some creepier cases—very astute observations, but those are still assumptions. All she's allowed to respond with is "truth" or "ass out of you and me" as quickly as she can. If she takes longer than three seconds or tries to explain herself, she gets a giant "BUZZ!" from the entire group, which is an impressive volume. She's been getting a lot of buzzes from the troupe.

"That's your natural color," Jade says.

"My hair?" Echo says. "Truth."

"BUZZ!" the group sounds out.

"You love our town," Big Mike says.

"Ass out of you and me!" Echo retorts.

"Your boyfriend is an ass but really gets you," Johnson, Eric Johnson says.

"Some truth but ass out of you and me," Echo fires off.

"BUZZ!" they sound in harmony, to remind her to stick to the format.

"You are an only child," Jimmy says.

"Ass out of you and me," Echo says.

"You read business books to feel smart," Johnson, Eric Johnson fires off.

"Truth."

"You are afraid of your own greatness," Big Mike says.

"Truth."

"You want to leave us," Jade says.

"Ass out of you and me."

"You have been assuming there are only two options about staying or going," Big Mike says.

"Truth."

"You need something you aren't getting from yourself," Jade says.

"Truth."

"You are afraid to take a leap of faith," Jimmy says.

"Truth."

"It's time to leave but you don't want to do it alone," Big Mike says.

Tearfully Echo says, "Truth."

"You are outgrowing your container," Jade says.

"Truth."

"You are going to leave to go to study drama," Johnson, Eric Johnson, says.

"Ass out of you and me."

"You have been assuming you have to create alone," Jade says.

"Truth."

"You would rather us help you."

"I love you guys." Jade was crying now.

"BUZZ!" they all say in unison.

So much of creative confidence is hatched in practice. There's an excellent volume on it by the Kelley brothers called *Creative Confidence.*[26] Another volume that's worth a read. You see Echo's largest assumption was *how might I?* rather than *how might we?* It's always better to create with council or tribe. *Tribes*[27] by Seth Godin is another swell read, too.

There's an old saying that comes from the indigenous groups of North America, "It takes a

[26] Kelley, T., & Kelley, D. (2015). *Creative Confidence: Unleashing the creative potential within us all*. London: W. Collins.

[27] Godin, S. (2012). *Tribes: We need you to lead us*. London: Piatkus.

village to raise a chief." It makes sense to me because who should the chief know better than the village he or she is serving? And as we uncovered earlier, design and storytelling both are about an exchange with an audience. They are both fundamentally service-oriented. Echo decides to learn vulnerability and takes a chance, because according to the inspirational quote by Brené Brown, that's the birthplace of innovation, creativity, and change. She invites people over.

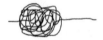

"Got any more of those waffles?" Jimmy asks, emerging from the kitchen presumably having eaten the last of her past. "Nevermind, I can see you have that mad scientist look you get, I'll just make something for us."

Echo stands reading, looking at a notebook, while Jade and Big Mike sit in her living room and wait. Johnson, Eric Johnson had a couple of errands to run and was going to reach out afterward to see if everyone was still going.

"Okay, okay! I found it!" She reads her notes aloud, "The rules for an ideation hackathon:

1) Start with assumption killing.
2) Stay in *yes/and* at all times.
3) Assume similarity in co-creation.
4) Silence is okay, it breeds courage.
5) Listen more than you speak.
6) Don't solve problems with answers.
7) Question everything, creativity goes.
8) The only bad idea is to kill ideas.

"These are great," Big Mike said, "are these all yours? I mean did you come up with them?"

"They are a work in progress," Echo said.

"We all are Echo! Fresh pancakes in a jiff!" Jimmy yelled from the kitchen.

"I'm going to miss you all so much," Echo said.

"Ass out of you and me," Jade said, smiling, and grabbed a marker and a 2x2. "Let's make sure we can see your design," Jade said, and placed it under Echo's "how might I" ... though the "I" had been crossed out to say, "we."

The crew ate pancakes and engaged in the third phase of the design thinking process, brainstorming, like the end of the world was coming and they could solve it with their ideation alone. They imagined and hacked and killed assumptions with better questions. They all had realizations at different points. Echo sat back and watched a *yes/and* build and escalate between Jimmy and Johnson, Eric Johnson, who'd made it after all. Big Mike and Jade moved and stood next to Echo, Jade holding something behind her back. "You assumed you couldn't take us with you because you'll always be here with us. But it's time," Jade said, brandishing a paper bag for Echo.

"But it's time," Echo echoed in her laughter.

4.

echo

builds

worlds

a quote
of new
journeys:

"every act of creation is first an

act of destruction."

pablo picasso

4.

I think the only difference between creation and reaction is our perspective. People assume that the opposite of creation is destruction. I am not one of these people. I see the antonym of creation as reaction. It's like Bizarro Superman, Superman's arch nemesis from Bizarro World. It was a place very much like earth but off in almost every way. When I was a kid, Thursdays in elementary school were what we called "opposite day," it was one day a week you could tell people you liked that you hated them so long as you yelled, "Opposite Day!" afterward. You see why humans are my spirit animal? So weird.

Creation and reaction have the exact same letters that compose the two words. It's simply a matter of seeing them in a different order, it changes everything. In other words, meaning changes with every change of our perspective. It's a dangerous thing, to create rather than react. It's easy to react. We have a saying in storytelling, in narrative design, that there exist in the world really only two fundamental stories.

1) A person goes on a journey.
2) A stranger comes to town.

Either can be told or designed as a reactive story or a creative story (same letters again, crazy huh?). This is where someone's POV or rules of world or worldview shine through the storylines or the designs. So far, we've observed as Echo has gone from a reactive state as the stranger in town to now being on the cusp of being the person going on the journey and happening to life rather than life happening to her.

In the last chapter, we ideated in brainstorm-ville. We learned ways to kill assumptions, too. What's interesting about brainstorming is that most people don't do it from a place of assumption clearing first. But I think we enter into the fourth space of the design thinking, storytelling, or narrative design space with so much more clarity and less blockage than we otherwise would have taking that extra step.

This fourth step is called prototyping in the design thinking methodologies, world creation in narrative design, or authoring in storytelling. We are going to see what ideas Echo decided to move forward with after her ideation jam sesh.

how might we gain creative confidence and live our dreams sooner rather than later?

Echo painted over it with a roller and then moved to another area and wrote:

how might we practice creative confidence and live our dreams sooner rather than later?

Echo stood back and looked at the new sentence. Yes, *better*, she thought. She looked around her house. It had been two weeks since her ideation session with her friends.

It had taken that long to arrange a place to stay, to tie up loose ends, take her money out of savings, and pack up her belongings. She sought out her leather chair and sunk into it. *Sigh.*

Echo didn't know what to expect next. But that was, in many ways, the epic nature of this phase. She thought about that and mouthed the word *prototyping*. She was growing to love the processes in design thinking, even if she found some of them kind of limiting. But that was something she would have to take up once her prototyping was finished.

She was world-building right now. The major fears she had around moving off to a massive city, like NYC, and attending some ridiculously cool place like Parsons School of Design, land of the best of the best of designers, was … well … terrifying. Plus, she didn't have the money to make the big one yet.

She'd read in *The $100 Startup*[28] to keep it small and test, test, test. She'd also recently read that every iPhone was a prototype. *Why would they want to perfect it, then they'd have nothing to release every year*, she noted. In *The $100 Startup*, it mentioned staying lean to stay responsive, agile, and creative. In fact, she thought that intimated that if you could bake that into a culture's DNA, then you'd likely once scaling need way less capital.

She couldn't wait for the movers to come grab these boxes. She couldn't wait to start her

---

[28] Guillebeau, C. (2015). *The $100 Startup*. London: Pan Books.

prototype tomorrow. She was also excited to start class next week. Echo decided that what she wanted to build up to was moving to NYC, attending Parsons, and eventually starting her own firm.

But her lean prototype was simply a move across town in walking distance to the local community college. She needed the move because she sold her car, of course; she kept the dreamcatcher, though. She was going to take some classes in design. They didn't have any offerings in strategy, or design thinking, or even in storytelling. But they did have some graphic design, creative writing, film and video, and interior design. She enrolled in all of them.

She was also downsizing. She'd decided to share an apartment with her friend from high school, Amanda. That was the one piece of the prototype that she hadn't planned very well. Echo liked having her own space to retreat to and, frankly, despite the growth, once an introvert, always an introvert.

But to save for NYC she needed the roommate and the smaller place. *Keep it lean $100 Startup*, she told herself. *Maybe this was a bad idea. She* *should probably just move, go for it. Maybe she was being a coward?* she wondered.

So many people are in a hurry, though. What was it that Big Mike had said? Oh, no, it wasn't Big Mike, it was Peter!

When she'd first started training at the Waffle House, she was rushing and broke some mugs and spilled some coffee. Peter helped her clean it up and simply said, "You're rushing it, Echo. I know you want to look like all the other waitstaff. But you won't, you're new. You have to go s-s-slow to g-g-go fast."

You have to go slow to go fast. It's also a mistake that too many founders make of their start-ups, too.

She was bored.

She should sleep but she wasn't tired.

The testing of her prototyping would begin tomorrow and if she were to be honest, she was feeling a little apprehensive. *But this was a long game*, she told herself.

She got up and moved over to a corner of the room where she had rolled up all of the 2x2s. She sat down in front of them and began unrolling them one by one. She had an idea. *She was going to go bias hunting!*

Geeking out, Echo moved back all of her furniture and created as much space as she could on her living room floor.

Then she finished unrolling all of the 2x2s and began creating a patchwork quilt on the floor. Once she'd laid them all out, she jumped up on the sofa and began pacing back and forth into the squishy cushions.

She observed, sleuthed, and searched for patterns. *I'm getting my clustering*[xiii] *on*, she thought with a grin. She started to see a pattern emerging slowly and then it would recede again. She hopped off the sofa and grabbed some post-it notes and a marker. Then she hopped back up onto the sofa and paced, staring into the 2x2s on the floor before her. She was double-checking her work, looking for a pattern she missed.

If she were to be honest, something didn't feel quite right about the prototype and she couldn't quite pinpoint what it was … and tomorrow the testing started. *Think, think, think, Echo, think … no … feel, feel, feel, Echo, feel. What doesn't feel right?* Her eye was drawn to a group of post-it notes that had been clustered on her first annual pancake ideation jam. *Won't be my last*, she mused, *I plan to institute that in my firm.*

"BOOM!" she yelled, jumped off the sofa, and landed near a 2x2 which she almost slipped on. She crouched down and started looking more closely at the ideas that had been grouped under "GAIN CREATIVE CONFIDENCE" and it hit her as she looked at all of them.

Every idea emanated from the single assumption that she didn't have creative confidence. It assumed a starting point from a place of lack. She had then gone and built her entire prototype based on that assumption.

She crawled over to the other 2x2s from the first annual pancake ideation jam. How might we live our dreams sooner rather than later … every single idea was predicated on the assumption that she had to start small. She had to build up to Parsons.

She hopped back up on the sofa. She'd just made a whole prototype; a whole user plan she was about to roll out tomorrow. But she hadn't gathered feedback, real feedback from her primary user – *herself*! She was no better than Apple, going into production with a prototype that hadn't been user-tested. She had assumed that she needed to commit to it in real life to see whether it worked. But that's not a lo-fi prototype.

What had happened?

Suddenly she knew, and it broke her heart. She was enjoying her friends so much that she pulled back at the last second in her prototyping. She let the safe idea win out. She decided it was all based on a lack of confidence in herself. She built her prototype inside an assumption that she had neglected to murder … the assumption that she was not enough.

I am enough.

She looked back up at the wall and saw her latest message barely dried:

how might we practice creative confidence and live our dreams sooner rather than later?

She grabbed the paint roller and dipped it into the wall-colored gallon of paint. She rolled over it. Something had clicked in her clustering. She'd rooted out the last of her assumptions in a user test. Now, she walked to a dry place on the wall and she took a breath and wrote in huge letters:

I practice

creative confidence

by living my dreams

now.

echo

sets

fires

"practice

creative confidence

by living your dreams"

echo

5.

The funny thing about prototypes is that when we don't test them first, we run the risk of testing them on the wrong crowd, inadvertently.

Let me explain … no … no, there is too much, let me summate:

I once spent a million dollars. I made a feature film and feature films are expensive. At the time, I was an artist, so much so, I would have called myself an *artiste* (← insert too-thick French accent and give yourself a look of disdain from me). I made a hit … on the surface. We won a whole bunch of festivals and fans all over the world seemed to love it. It seemed destined for greatness. We had a deal with Warner Bros. and I somehow managed in all my kind-ego *(I'm too empathic for a mean-ego)* at the time to have a clarified enough voice that I could retro-match my voice to an audience out there.

But there was a large problem. There had been some big assumptions and unlike Echo I didn't catch it before employing over 150 people to spend over a million bucks on a movie.

The audience was varied and disparate and not seemingly connected into one marketable group. And so the film followed suit. It fell into marketing no-persons' land.

While it definitely had a *thematic* point of view or constructed narrative, it did not have a genre point of view. It was what we call a dramedy and this was before that was a thing. Critics said it was too family-friendly to be indie and families didn't like how we used certain words and that the content was too edgy for kids.

Essentially, we made a film that everyone thought was for someone else. We made it firmly in the creative friend zone. This is what happens when prototypes are built out of hidden assumptions. This is also why it's become part of my teaching credo and creative mantra to shoot assumptions in the forehead and then in the heart for good measure. I am not a violent person; I'm the guy that feels bad for clothes that I have that don't get worn or rodents in the pantry just trying to be warm in winter, but I will kill the shit out of some assumptions.

Because, like black widow spiders (that's the other exception I make), they will kill you and yours without even thinking.

I'm grateful that Echo didn't make that same mistake. She'd made a few assumptions. One of them was the assumption that she made as the subject of her clustering and re-clustering frenzy, that she was designing assuming that her user ... was at a disadvantage and not an equal partner in the design exchange. When we do this, we run the sincere risk of allowing ego to run the show and design the day. We believe ourselves to be the enlightened and our disadvantaged user to not know what's good for them. But whether we like it or not, as creators in this design or narrative design or storytelling world, we serve at the pleasure of the consumer. David Ogilvy (considered the father of advertising as we know it) once said that if it doesn't sell, it isn't creative.

He believed a form of the customer is always right. I think it's a hybrid approach, personally. The customer is always your best test of whether you're right. We create and we iterate. We grow and then we change. Sometimes the customer didn't know that they wanted an automobile because it didn't exist yet. I think we have an obligation as design thinkers, strategists, storytellers, narrative designers, or whatever we call ourselves to think past people wanting a faster horse but still serving them rather than us. The idea that Ford served the customer need, even if his solution created an alternative, and ultimately more viable, future.

That said, every solution creates more problems. I'm not sure horse flatulence would have had the same emissions as automobiles. Then again, they say that cattle and their flatulence are the biggest offender in terms of greenhouse gases on the planet. So, maybe I'm wrong.

That's just it though, isn't it? We have to be so comfortable in the polarity of right and wrong that we realize we are always both at the same time. Being one hundred percent right or one hundred percent wrong or one hundred anything, for that matter, isn't really a thing we human beings do well. What we are good at is change and changing. We aren't always very epic at managing those changes or knowing how we fit into life after our growth spurts, but we do morph well. We are all born with the inherent gift of shapeshifting, my indigenous grandmother would say. Some have the will to use the ability for the world and some use it to hide from the world. We are ultimately at a crossroads as to which we will do. Will we hide our dreams from the world or share them through our pursuits? Will we share our care of the things we love in life or hide behind them as a refuge from the big, bad world?

Well, as Jim Rohn, mentor of Tony Robbins, says, "Whether you think you can or can't, you're right."

I have a habit of looking up people I admire to see if I can find what they read or who they studied under. Then, I go and find those books and materials to see if I come to some of the same conclusions or take a different path. Well, in a way, that's what Echo is doing now. She not only saw the writing on the wall, she effing put it there and now she's en fuego.

side note:

en fuego means on fire,

and on fire is a slang term

for someone in badassery

157

Echo was lost again.

It had been several weeks and still she was getting lost. *Maybe she was rushing*, she thought. But she'd been actively trying to go slow to go fast, and so far, slow was all she could muster. At first, the shock to the system was only made bearable by the serendipity of the whole thing. *1101, 1103, 1105, 1107, 1109, 1111 ... where the hell was 1113?*

This was the second time she'd circled this square and still not found 1113. She retraced her steps and *no*. She went around the corner and looked up and down and *no*.

A guy just passed behind her and she turned to see him walking rapidly away. She pursued. "Excuse me, excuse me?" she mousily tried to mumble his attention.

He kept walking. It was at this point she usually thought people were rude and that the world was full of a-holes. But since being in NYC, she had been making attempts to *assume* that it was something she was doing or not doing. *Not that everything was her fault or ever would be* … No, Echo was just attempting to take charge of the things she could change and let go of the ones that she couldn't. She was attempting to take charge of creating her life with confidence.

She remembered something her sister would always shout, "When you're that quiet, Echo, it makes me want to yell! JUST TO BALANCE OUT THE VOLUME! Speak up, sis."

"Hey there, guy walking away from me!"

She felt like she was shouting. But really, she had a hunch that she was simply playing the music of her voice at a reasonable volume. He stopped. He waited. *Maybe he is waiting to see if the voice was talking to him? Or whether he was just yelled at? Or if he should be offended?*

She had also noticed that as she began to live into her dreams, she noticed more and more areas of herself that didn't fit into them. Things like all the self-talk. She saw more and more clearly through the couraging she was engaging in that the creating out of a place of lack that almost kept her in place was coming from inside her and not outside her. *There's no one to blame for self-talk*, she thought. She said, "Ahoy there, matey."

Ahoy there, matey? Nope. Self-talk. But COME ON!

He turned around, grinning at that. He turned slowly and deliberately. It reminded her of something. She couldn't tell what just yet.

"Ahoy there, yourself, landlubber. Is it because I'm Australian that you assume I'm a pirate?" He winked, kindly letting her comment off the hook.

Her face turned pale. The serendipity had been swell up to now and focused mostly in getting her life in alignment with her intentions. But this was absurd. The universe was being … was being … a …

"Silly goose," he said.

"Silly goose," Echo ehoed.

"Yea, you betcha. You must think I'm a right silly goose going straight into all that extra pirate talk. I mean yours, yours was a gas. Mine? Overkill. But you were trying to get my attention. I assume you are lost?" He noted the paper in her hand.

She nodded.

"1113? Design and Management? Am I right? It happened to me, too, a couple of years ago. I wandered and circled around and around this damn square way too many times. Who do you have?"

"Roberts," she said.

"Oh, he'll be fine. I didn't have him in that class, but I hear his section's the most fun. He's a storyteller, that one. I've got him in narrative design. If he teaches them similarly, then you'd better get ready to participate, whether you think you want to or not. He tends to pull it out of you. It's great, though, once you get past all the fireside chats about creating a safe space together as a class. That's a bit mush for someone from the bush."

A pause.

"Will you say something? I feel like I'm saying way too much about not much." He looked nervous now. She took that in, took him in.

"Where are you from?" she asked.

"Australia, I already said …"

"No, before that, or after that, or in between, I mean?" Now she felt foolish.

"I'm not sure what you are getting at? And honestly, I can't tell if you're playing a joke on me," he said.

It's official, Echo thought, *everyone has self-talk*. Echo said, "It's okay, this is a safe space," and smiled at him something genuine.

He smiled back, "Graceful segue, 1113 is around the corner you just came from, so go back around there, but snag a sharp and hook-like left straight away."

"You could just walk me," Echo said.

"Famous last words," he said, while they walked, "here we are, 1113."

"I don't see how I walked past it so many times. It seems so obvious now," Echo said.

"Good design always seems obvious after. I'm Ari," he said.

"I know, we were in fifth grade together," Echo said, and walked into the classroom.

Something Ari said to Echo is wonderfully true about anything good, I suspect, but certainly about design and storytelling. The people that have it truly mastered do them with an ease that doesn't ever alert you to the fact that a story was told or that a design took place.

But you felt the experience. It impacted you. And in rare cases, it changes everything for you.

Clint Eastwood does two things on his sets when directing that I love deeply. One, he never says action. He believes it's the equivalent of someone telling a runner to run or hungry person to eat. He understands that the best of actors of their craft do not need to be told, rushed, or jolted at the beginning of bringing something to life.

I think we tend to do this in managing our own creativity as well. We yell at ourselves to perform, instead of what Eastwood tells his actors, "Whenever you're ready." I love this so much. It allows us to surf the waves of creativity to get on top of the wave rather than simply jumping on our board regardless of what the ocean is doing right then and, make no mistake, creativity is an ocean, with its own non-terrestrial world of life and currents and weather.

The second thing that Eastwood does on set that I am in love with is very meta. He directs the film with the intention to make something for the audience to experience. He believes that if he does his job well, they will never notice the director in the film, but rather be taken on a grand adventure with the story and the people, the actors, living that story for each of us.

I think there are many kinds of creatives in the world and I am one of these that believes every human to be fundamentally creative. Now, some may choose accounting and linear worlds of science and STEM over circular stories and the fine arts. But I think the idea of faith is fundamentally creative and it's the most essential part of being human. It's the reason humans are my spirit animal. We are irrational in our belief that we are rational. We seek to build systems and run operations and grow ourselves, our endeavors, our companies, our projects, even our children, with the irrational belief in meaning that is our inherent faith. Even those that claim to believe in meaninglessness still believe in something.

We take that creativity and apply it to the thoughts, hopes, dreams, and imaginations in our own potential. This, at its core, is our birthright, creative confidence. It's what we've evolved into in order to propagate our species and build our world into something special.

I'm excited about the future. Because it's us and I'm excited about us, you and me. I think we're about to get nuts and it's going to be a phenomenal story. We may have rushed through Echo's prototype and her testing in the last chapter. But that's by narrative design.

Her original prototype was crap.

She didn't really—despite all the whys—dig deep enough to know that she was enough. She already had creative confidence; it was simply a matter of redirecting energy she used on things like: confidently believing in the construct that the dashed-yellow lines in the road keep other drivers from crashing into her car into something else. Like: it's for me to pursue my passions, because those fires are in me to light the world.

That was a doozy, I know, UBER-CHEESE, but it's needed for the design of the next section.

Echo felt like she'd taken too many minutes getting to class, and then too many minutes getting loudly situated. She could feel Professor Roberts noticing. She assumed he was irritated. She would be. *Ass out of you and me!* she heard Big Mike in her thoughts and smiled.

They'd given her a big send-off from the last show they did together. *Whew*, finally she was ready to take notes. She had her pen and papers and sticky notes, and even a folded 2x2 in her backpack. She took a sip of water from her water bottle, never noticing until now that the lid made quite a squeaky sound.

She tried to set it down slowly and quietly. *Just set the water bottle down slowly and nobody gets hurt.*

Professor Roberts smiled at her, noticing her intentional movements. He looked familiar, too. Then she looked at the board, *the dreamcatcher. NO!* This was all starting to feel like she was in someone else's story. She needed to take back control somehow. She'd wait her turn. For now, she just observed and learned.

"Has anyone heard of the book *The Design Way*?" A couple of hands shot up. Echo mouthed something silently. Professor Roberts noticed. This guy was crazy observant. *Oh, empaths*, she mused. *Yep, and Ari, too.*

"You, how about you, I assume you're Echo?"

"Ass out of you and me," shot out of her mouth before her hands could cover it fast enough. Laughter followed.

"For real. You're right about that. I did assume. Apologies," he said, chuckling, "you were also mouthing something and while I'm not a lip-reader, I'm pretty certain you weren't rehearsing your auto-reply to the word *assume*," he said.

More laughter. She was going to like this class.

She thought a moment, *what had she been mouthing? It was when he mentioned the book. Oh!* She blurted out, "Humans did not discover fire, they designed it."

"Yes!" he said, and went to the chalkboard and wrote it up there, though he changed the word "they" to "we."

Then he underlined the word "we" several times. "I made one build, yes *they* did, and *we* will. I simply moved us from the past to the present with an implied future."

"Yah, simply," Echo said, and covered her mouth again. Everyone laughed in agreement.

"Echo, you don't have to cover your voice up here. If you want, this is where you'll design it. Who can tell me what a *voice* is in design or even better, narrative design, which you lovely people will not have taken yet?"

No one raised their hand. Echo hesitated. She started to raise her hand slowly.

"Has anyone ever been to Casa Bonita?"

A hand shot up. "Yes!" a young man with a ball cap said. "I'm from Denver! Love that place."

"It was pretty easy for him to say that, wasn't it?"

The class nodded in unison. "And my Casa Bonita friend, Aiden, was it? How did you signal the waitstaff while at the pretty house?"

"Ooh, you raise these little flags and then someone knows you want service."

"Again, the excitement over the experience is palpable. Did anyone else notice that?" Professor Roberts asked.

Lots of nods and mutterings of yes came from the other students.

"Why was it easy for Aiden to talk about Casa Bonita? Anyone? No flag raising, no hands up, just tell me and learn to have an ideating session by listening to one another. Go on, speak your minds."

"He clearly loved it," a young woman with purple hair said.

"Right, and that made it easy to talk about because he felt so much for it," another young woman stated.

"I noticed that he wasn't as enthusiastic about the flag raising, though," a young man noted.

"Is that true, Aiden?" Professor Roberts asked.

"I don't know. I know that I could never get them to come to the flag when I wanted extra sopapillas," he said, to the laughter of everyone.

"What's a sopapilla?" another student asked.

"Oooh, are you kidding me? You don't know what a sopapilla is? Only the greatest fried puff pastry on the planet!" Aiden was leaning forward in his chair.

The class laughed.

Professor Roberts countered, "You've never had my mama's fry bread. Going to have to agree to disagree until your world experience has grown."

More laughter.

Professor Roberts continued, "It's interesting that he came alive again, isn't it? So, what can we assume the experience was like when no one would answer the call of the raised flag?"

"Disappointing," one student said.

"Frustrating," said another.

"Silencing," someone said.

Roberts turned around in a flash. "Who said that?"

Echo replied, "Me."

"Astute, Echo, very astute. What is the opposite of being silenced, Echo?"

"Speaking up."

Roberts nodded thoughtfully, then asked, "Why did the little boy Aiden—Aiden, I assume you were a little boy the last time you went—wait, when was the last time you went to Casa Bonita?"

"Right before I moved here five weeks ago," he said, blushing.

The class burst into laughter.

Roberts looked at Echo. "Ass out of you and me, ha! Beat you to it."

More laughter.

"Okay, folks, seriously now that you're awake, why did teenage or early 20s Aiden feel so downtrodden when he couldn't get anyone to listen to him with his freak flag of flavor flying high?"

"He loves sopa … sopa … sopa …" a student couldn't finish. Another helped, "Sopapillas." The first continued, "Yes! He loves these sopapillas and no one would listen."

"BOOM!" Roberts said. "Okay, and now … Echo … why is this important? What does it make us think if we continually ask for what we deeply love and don't get it?"

"That we don't have a say ..." she got it, "that we don't have a voice."

"Yahtzee! Write this down people, because it will be on a quiz if I decide to do quizzes for the first time this year. Rephrase it and say it like it should be on a test, Echo," Roberts said.

Echo smiled. "When we don't have a say, we forget we have a voice."

"Deep," Roberts said sincerely.

"Or! When we don't say what we love, we don't have a voice," Echo said.

"Wise," Roberts said, sincerely. "Write it down. Good things come in threes, Echo. Reframe it in an active rather than reactive way."

Echo took a breath and said, "Our voice is the fire we design, the love we share through what we make in the world."

I've been working in narrative design for years now. Developing it, growing it, overthrowing it, and starting over with it. I've gone through so many iterations I can't even count. I'm into imaginary numbers now. But one thing has held true in the core of these concepts, and as I apply and metamorphize the work even more, having a voice is key to creating any work.

I love that phrase that Echo brought out from *The Design Way* because it speaks so eloquently to something it's not even talking about. It's literally speaking about physical fire and the design of it coming from humanity rather than the old Prometheus story. But I've always liked that Prometheus story, too. And for the same reason that I enjoy this quote, *"Humans did not discover fire, they designed it."*

Prometheus stole away to give mankind the secret to making fire, a secret kept by the gods. It's funny because in many of the old myths and religious stories of mankind, someone is always sneaking off from deity cabin at camp ain't-easy-being-human and giving the campers smokes or in this case the secret of fire or in the case of Adam and Eve the ability to do *either/or*, good/evil, right/wrongs … etc. You get the idea. I think in the case of Prometheus, I always saw it as someone trying to gift us with the secret to passion ... warmth.

I think the fire is our analogy for our passion, the feelings behind our voice. We design that. We construct our deeper dreams through that same passion and those become the vessels for our voice in the world, the tinder and firewood for the flames of our time here on earth.

There's little we can do in the world of note without having a voice.

In my work with storytellers of all kinds and designers of all kinds, I continue to see this through line. We are the stories we believe about ourselves. We live the designs we make for ourselves. And unlike other beasts, we irrational beings, we humans, we animals struggling with consciousness, can design our fire to burn anywhere, anytime, in any weather, and in any context. We can design our lives, our stories.

When we do this, we are passion with skin on. And our world is in dire need of it.

Echo sat in the lunchroom at Parsons School of Design on 5th Avenue in New York City thinking about student loans and sushi. She sat at a bar top table that was looking out at 12th Street. She was watching people coming and going out of a little place called the Garden of Eden. She could barely see something hanging from the ceiling in the store and couldn't make it out properly. She decided that after class on her walk back to the dorms, she would inspect this phenomenon.

She placed some ginger on her spicy tuna sushi and dipped it into the soy sauce. She saw Ari from afar and waved. He motioned to ask if he could come join her and she shrugged.

He couldn't tell what she was answering and so beside deciding they would be miserable charades partners, he came over to ask her if he could sit by her.

"Do you mind if I sit?"

Echo nodded.

"You do mind? Or I can sit?"

"Just sit down, Ari."

"You're Echo, aren't you?"

"Good memory."

"I phoned a friend. My mum. I asked her to Facebook our old teacher. My mum is Facebook friends with her ..." Ari said, and waited.

They both simultaneously said, "Mrs. Carson."

"Okay, up until that moment I wasn't sure if you were an imposter. Now I know it's you," he flirted.

"Imposter? I don't know," she said, taking a bite of sushi, "I'm feeling a little impostery around here. I mean, look at where we are!"

Ari laughed and glanced down at the book Echo was reading.

"What?" she asked, and looked at the book, too.

"You're reading that? It's not in your classwork yet. I know, because I'm an upperclassman and you're a freshman, freshwoman, excuse me."

She was reading Idris Mootee's book *Design Thinking for Strategic Innovation*.[29]

"They didn't have it at my library. I went through this quarter-life crisis last year, okay, six months ago, and redesigned everything. I looked for every book on design thinking I could find, which mostly consisted of those with design thinking in the title and there weren't many. Even less that I could get my hands on. So, I raided the library here on day one. Have you read this one?" She handed him the book.

"Imposter my arse," he said, taking the book from her and looking it over. "Yes, I have, it's a good one. Maybe one of the most practical applications. What'd you think of 1113?" He handed her the book back.

"Kind of great. He's a little different, but it was cool how easy it was to speak up," she said.

---

[29] Mootee, I. (2013). *Design Thinking for Strategic Innovation: What They Can't Teach You at Business or Design School*. Hoboken, NJ: John Wiley & Sons.

"That doesn't seem like it would ever be a problem for you," he said, "but yeah, that's kind of one of his things, collaboration."

Echo was shocked. "That doesn't seem like that would ever be a problem for you," she echoed.

"Yeah, I mean you've got so much confidence, like you're in the *Flow* all the time," he said.

"Is that like a *Kung Fu* reference?"

"Well, good for you knowing about *Kung Fu* and not the panda. Though, if I'm honest, I've watched all three back-to-back. But no, not any of the *Kung Fu*s, it's a book reference for a book called *Flow*,[30]" he said.

tip:

you can learn all you need to know about working in creativity by watching old episodes of kung fu

---

[30] Csikszentmihalyi, M. (2009). *Flow: The Psychology of Optimal Experience*. New York: Harper Row.

"I'd highly recommend you added it to your list."
Echo pulled out a small *Cavallini Papers* journal
with an old scientific diagram of a brain in good
health and took notes on the book suggestion.

"I like that journal," Ari said.

"It was all I could afford at the Strand
Bookstore, which is the greatest place on earth,"
Echo said, putting away her little notebook.

"There's a whole used section and there are used
books everywhere, I can show you, it's actually
one of the most affordable places in town," Ari
said. "What are you doing now?"

"I was about to go and do observations for an
empathy map[xiv] on a business. I was thinking
about going to the Garden of Eden," she said.

"What about the Strand? They have customers
you can observe as well," he said.

"If you can answer two questions correctly, Ari,"
she said playfully.

"I'm up for the challenge," he said.

"The first is, would this be a date?" she asked. She couldn't believe how comfortable she felt at this school and with these people. That said, the professor and Ari had been in the dreamcatcher. They were personas she designed with.

"Of course, and the second question?" he asked.

"The second is: do you know what's hanging on the ceiling at the deli across the street?"

"Yes."

"And?" she asked, noticing the, *"yes/and"* between them.

"I'll show you on our way. You should see things for yourself," he said, and held out his hand.

"Great answer, matey," she said.

A year passed, and courses don't last. What started as autumn magic became winter chill and what began as living the dream became common. That's what happens when confidence blooms.

Echo found everything around her growing by the time spring came. She found herself growing, her feelings for Ari growing, her enjoyment of her life growing, but also the nagging growing.

Something needed to change, again.

Why don't things last? Why don't great things stay the same? She couldn't understand it or why this feeling seemed to be mounting. Her designs were sound. She'd put so much work into getting to Parsons, into all that surrounded it. Now, it didn't seem as special. There was something about it that she couldn't place, *no, that wasn't right*, something *about her she couldn't place.*

She needed to do an empathy map on herself, perhaps? That *Flow* that leads to creativity and then happiness, that wasn't anywhere to be found. It's possible she was just overtired. She'd been cramming so much into her skull hoping it would blossom in her heart. She didn't know exactly what she should do. Nothing was actually wrong on the surface. Intuitively, though, she knew she was off her game. The wake-up call came in the form of a professor asking her to stay after class for a check-in. Professor Rancourt was teaching an integrated studio, one of the times when it all comes together.

"Echo, I wanted to check in. I know it can be a lot to adjust to inside, the city, the school, all of us."

Echo saw it here, too, another empath. She let down her guard, recognizing kindred.

"It's technically all great, Professor Rancourt."

"But …"

"Something's missing. I think maybe I expected too much," Echo said.

"Hmmm. Maybe. Or maybe you're not expecting enough."

"What do you mean?" Echo asked, surprised.

"Why did you come here?" the professor asked.

"To practice creative confidence safely," Echo said.

"Why safely?" Rancourt asked.

"I was too shy to try otherwise," Echo shared.

"Why were you shy, Echo?" Rancourt asked.

"I wasn't in touch with my voice," Echo replied.

"Why's your voice matter?" the professor asked.

"It's my way to set the world on fire," she said.

"Why does fire need safety?" Rancourt asked.

"Why does fire need safety?" Echo echoed.

"It may just need a container," Rancourt offered.

So often we assume, *ass out of you and me*, we need safety when we are feeling unsafe. But how is that assumption any different than assuming we need a chair because we feel tired of standing?

We may not need a chair at all, just a place to sit. Assumptions, we've discussed a great deal, but they are a funny thing and they are just as constant as creativity.

Because they are as intrinsic to the human experience as feeling, creativity, faith, or doubt. In fact, in many ways they lay the foundation for each of the human experiences. They are at their best context setters and at their worst context setters. Meaning that if we assume we will fail we set a context just as much as assuming we will succeed sets a context.

My favorite story about the assumptions is in the tale of the set of identical twins and the science experiment:

The goal was to find identical twins with opposite tendencies toward outlooks on life.

After much searching and researching, the scientists in charge found a couple of kiddos in Minnesota. The parents agreed to the experiment if the scientists would conduct their behavioral experiment on the family's property.

Seeing no harm in agreeing to the children's comfortability, the team agreed and set up their operation in the family's old wooden barn.

The barn had two stalls only and of equal size. Each had a door with a half-door that could open to the outside for stalled animals to enjoy fresh sunshine. The scientists saw these as ideal for observation.

So, they had each twin make a list. On the lists were every toy either sibling had ever dreamed of owning. As you can imagine, the lists were long and rivaled any Christmas list on earth. The twins handed over their lists to the scientists.

Now, in their testing the scientists had revealed what they had most hoped to find; one twin was an absolute optimist and the other a fundamental pessimist. They patted each other on the back when they uncovered this, equal and opposite actions and reactions and all that bluster.

The day of testing came.

The scientists were up early that morning with their assistants and filling each stall. One stall had been filled with the list of the optimist down to every toy. The other was filled a child's chest high with horseshit.

The pessimist was invited into the stall full of toys to play. The optimist was tossed head first into the pile of horseshit. Within moments, the scientists were drawn to the crying in the stall with all the toys.

In it a child sat in supreme melancholy. The sadness permeated the air around the twin. The scientists made some notes and then one ventured to ask, "Why are you crying, little one?"

"I don't know what to play with," came the reply. *Whack!* Shit hit a scientist in the face. *Whack! Whack!* More shit flew and hit more of the observers.

Another that had yet to be hit with the poo assumed the child was being vindictive and opened his mouth to reprimand the twin, only to take a turd in the teeth. "It hit my mouf, it hit my teef, it's in my mouf!" was all he could dance around and say.

Speaking of dancing around, it was the dancing, the laughter, and the pure joy that finally drew the cautious observers over to the other stall that was becoming less full of shit by the moment.

Thud! A poo hit the wall of the stall.

One of the observers asked, "Child, why are you so happy? You asked for a list of gifts and they were given to someone else, you've been handed nothing but doo-doo."

The twin stopped momentarily with a brightness and fire for life in his eyes that could have no place for anything base; there was no vindictiveness, no vengeance, and they began taking notes.

The optimistic twin thought and then giggled, "Well, I just figured with this much horseshit, there's gotta be a pony under here somewhere!"

Life is what we make of it and while there may not be a pony under there, we could all use a little less shit in our lives. Meaning: getting clear is good work no matter what.

Echo approached the building for the event. It was the address that Professor Rancourt had given her a couple of days ago. The event was for *Green Light for Girls*,[31] a STEM meets design thinking non-profit for teen girls that Professor Rancourt had founded, who was herself a professed *"recovering engineer."*

Echo thought it was rad that she had been invited by one of her favorite profs to connect outside of school. She was greeted and then shown up to the event. Echo played inside subjects she'd discarded long ago with girls that seemed to be discovering the subjects for the first time.

She couldn't remember the last time she'd had this much fun at school, *not design school, but real school*, she thought, and stopped in her tracks. *When did I stop seeing school as school?* She ran through a swift rabbit hole exercise in her head. *It was when I became so career focused. I started looking to "get through" instead of "going through."* She looked around at the girls in the event. They were definitely experiencing joy for joy's sake, not learning for the sake of gaining knowledge or

---

[31] www.greenlightforgirls.org is an international organization dedicated to inspiring girls of all ages and backgrounds in STEM subjects by introducing them to the world of science.

changing some outcome or trajectory, but instead straight up loving learning.

It reminded her of the questionable story that Professor Roberts had told in class about the twins and the science experiment. *When did I become the pessimist sitting with all of her dreams and pouting?* Echo wondered.

She was tapped on the shoulder by a young girl, maybe 14 years of age, with a name tag on that said Lavender. "That's a lovely name, Lavender," Echo said. "I have an unusual name, too." Echo pointed to her own name tag.

"Echo," Lavender read aloud, and laughed a pretty little trill of a sound. "That's a lovely name, too. So, you went to Parsons School of Design?"

"I'm still going actually. I'm in my second year. I'm in Miss Melissa's class," Echo said.

"That's awesome, I plan to either go to Harvard or Parsons, I haven't decided yet. But if I go to Parsons, I might go to the one in Paris."

"It's good to have plans. Just make sure you leave room to reiterate them, Lavender," Echo said, and felt the comment echo within herself.

She excused herself. The event was winding down and she had a mountain of work to get to and was planning to pour her way through it. Now, she wasn't sure what she'd do.

She watched as Professor Rancourt walked in her direction. "Hey there, Echo, wait up, before you go I wanted you to meet Lavender."

"Oh, I just did, lovely girl, big plans."

"She does have them. But she's also from a family where she may not get to do much past what she can pull off herself. It's a tough world out there when you have to teach yourself so much, isn't it?" the professor asked Echo.

"Yes, it is," Echo reflected.

She could see what Professor Rancourt meant about being out in the world, it's not necessarily a safe place. Your plans get messed with and what's more, so do your feelings. Echo could see so much of herself in the bright-eyed girl.

"I'm telling you, Ari, it was so weird. It's like I was looking at my own soul in that girl's eyes." Echo was laying with her head on Ari's shoulder as they watched the people coming and going from the deli across from Parsons.

"That must have been surreal," he said, playing with her hair.

"And then there was something the professor said: *It's a tough world out there when you have to teach yourself so much, isn't it?*" Echo echoed.

"Is that how you feel, Echo?" Ari asked.

"Yes."

"That sounds lonely," he said, and leaned down to kiss her forehead.

"It was. The thing is, it was a driver for so long. I'm not lonely now. And it's like, you know when I told you something felt off, I didn't feel like myself?" she asked.

"You mentioned that something was missing," Ari remembered.

"Yes! Well, I think it might just be my lonely survivalist identity."

Silence.

"That's deep, lady," Ari said.

"What should I do?" she asked.

"I'm not certain I've ever heard you ask that of anyone?" he said, surprised.

"Well?"

"I think that you've been giving to you for so long, and rightly so, because not many others have been, but maybe it's time to give to others just as intentionally as you designed for yourself. Maybe it's time you design for others, Echo," Ari said.

She felt herself almost echo his words and stopped herself. Instead she said, "I'm not in the paper bag anymore, Ari. I'm going to show others the way out."

"Design for them, Echo, set those bags on fire."

"I'm going to set fires," Echo said in her voice.

Echo redesigned her narrative and will continue to do so for many moons to come. She's moved into what Robert Kegan[32] calls a self-transformative mind. It's exactly what it sounds like. It's the ability in narrative design and design thinking, both, to synthesize insights into patterns of change and development. When you can synthesize, the sky is the limit. The connections you'll make between seemingly unrelated events, moments, and information will lead to insights that can instantly adapt your paradigm.

You'll become a mental model creator. Clustering won't just happen in the design or narrative

[32] Kegan, R. (1997). *In Over Our Heads: The Mental Demands of Modern Life*. Cambridge: Harvard Univ. Press.

process, but rather it won't really turn off. The Harvard Graduate School of Education, where Kegan teaches, uses the motto *Learn to Change the World*, and I've found that to be epically truer than we can imagine. Besides the fact that it's a double entendre which I nerdily and dearly love, it's the way forward. It harkens to the iterative mindset. Which I predict to be the very best hope for humanity to adapt to our rapidly changing world swiftly enough to both change with it and guide its currents of ever-shifting realities.

One of my favorite things about narrative design is that it doesn't solve problems. It's been said by many that design thinking is for problem-solving. I think where narrative design moves away from this mindset is when it goes to the narrative. It's not a problem-focused modality.

Instead, it works to find the roots of the belief systems that created the problem. Then, rather than solve for that problem, it looks to uproot or upend the problem through a narrative shapeshift. This process takes us to a place where it's possible to redesign the reality and watch the problem cease to be. It's a place where the problems we perceive are questions at their assumptive roots. I hold a firm belief, as do most strategic designers, storytellers, and creators that I know, that we don't have great answers because we don't ask great questions.

I'll leave you with that—ask great questions, it'll change the answers you receive. That and you should always remember what you do when you assume … thanks for taking the time to read.

t.s. eliot said

the end is

where we

start from...

so, start.

herd the cats:

they straight ran,
they scattered,
they made flan,
they scatted,

they read some jazz,
then, played some jazz,
those cats, those cool cats,
the cats of…

can we focus, geez?
our clients in Belize?
who said Belize?
can I be the one to travel, please?

they read some books,
they wrote some books,
they never, ever respond
to our dirty looks,
those cats.

about

jack roberts

"We become the story we tell.
That's why it's so vital to
 tell an authentic one."

Jack Roberts is the founder of **storylab**® a narrative design® firm dedicated to transforming the human story. He is the creator of narrative design®, the bestselling author of 23 books, including the upcoming *Echo Designs Her Way Out of a Paper Bag: How to Change Anything Using Design Thinking and Storytelling!),* as well as a published poet and the award-winning author of 7 screenplays. He is also an award-winning actor, producer, and production designer in feature film and television with 21 international awards to date.

Through **storylab**® Jack consults Global Top 100s and Fortune 50 companies on narrative design®, storytelling, data synthesis, innovation, change design, communication design, media design, and creative leadership. He earned a Global Executive Master's in Strategic Design and Management from Parsons School of Design in Paris in 2018. Jack teaches design, management, and storytelling during the summer at Parsons School of Design in New York. He's also an active voter and tribal citizen of the Cherokee Nation.

Conversational topics: anything that interests you, stories, horses, boats, presence, human evolution, the creative takeover, & raccoons versus bears.

this is a

glossary

of terms:

---

[i] Re-Story: the process of taking a narrative or belief and changing the nature of the emotions and assumptions around that story without altering the events at all.

[ii] Yes/And: a mental model that denotes acceptance and to shift utilizes redirection and/or building rather than opposition.

[iii] Silly Goose: is a pseudo-common idiom, often in use by parents of small children, inferring that the person in question needs to stop being nervous or childish and get the job done.

[iv] Empathizing: Learning about the audience for whom you are designing for, communicating to, and/or for whom you are creating.

[v] Dreamcatching: the process of empathizing in order to discern/uncover and clarify or sift the hopes and dreams of yourself and/or others.

[vi] Point of no return: something happens in which the hero/heroine of a story cannot go backwards. They decide on a path that closes the doors behind them. In a screenplay it will often take place at the mid-point, while in a narrative design framework it may take place once a point of view is established and the former assumptions guiding decision making have been murdered in a most foul manner.

[vii] Design constraint: limits to the actions of a design or point of view in the design, in some ways the design constraint is the next step after establishing a point of view which will likely be

based on the insights from empathizing with your audience or user.

viii Rules of world: refers to the guidelines or constraints to which a work of fiction must establish and adhere to for an integrated story to take place.

ix Iterative: the practice of always being in an ongoing process.

x Couraging: a *narrative design* term describing the practice of actively uncovering what you're afraid of even if there's nothing you can do about it in the immediate.

xi Ideation session: a focused brainstorming session in storytelling, design thinking, and narrative design* to generate as many ideas as physically possible, typically at least one hundred. *Narrative design also uses a value add-on called the 1-8-7 – it's a process to kill assumptions.

xii Empath: not to be confused with a psychic, an empath has such a high EQ, that is, Emotional Intelligence, they can sense, map, and respond to pattern recognition they observe in others' emotions in a similar fashion to someone with a high IQ and their ability to sense and recognize patterns in non-emotional data points. An empath is, simply put, an emotional genius.

xiii Clustering: in design thinking, it is the process of finding patterns in observations and research in order to draw insights into the users.

xiv Empathy map: a method of design thinking to better understand users, the map is a tool developed by strategyzer.com